Memoirs of a Field Officer – Graham Lean

MEMOIRS OF A FIELD OFFICER

Thailand, and the Boat People
1975-1985

Graham Lean

First published in 2023 by
Alatier Press, Edinburgh

Publishing services provided by Lumphanan Press
www.lumphananpress.co.uk

Text and Photographs © Graham Lean 2023

Printed and Bound by Imprint Digital, UK

ISBN: 978-1-7394341-0-6

These brief recollections were stirred into existence by my sister and brother-in-law, Bryony and Norman Malvenan, who urged me to make good a vague intention I had been harbouring to record them 'one day'. The book is dedicated to my daughter Alanna and son Tiernan, to give them some idea of how their father first arrived in the country of their birth, Thailand, and of his early experiences there as a young man working with the United Nations. My appreciation is therefore due to the family for providing both the catalyst and the inspiration for my modest efforts.

My thanks also to Colin Donald and James Bourne (first encountered in Bangkok and Singapore respectively) for sharing their professional experience as writers, for their reviews of the drafts, and their active encouragement. The writing process has been very rewarding in different and unexpected ways – reliving experiences and recovering both memories and emotions, even if some did not quite fit within the confines of the perspective I present in the pages that follow.

Graham Lean, Edinburgh, April 2023

Contents

Prologue

September 1975. The Singapore Airlines Boeing 747 flight from Bahrain to Singapore via Bangkok is climbing out of the heat of the desert, and I am looking forward to another chilled glass of the champagne that had been advertised so effectively. I have a window seat on the starboard side above the wing, so am perfectly placed to witness the outer starboard engine emit a flash, then burst into flames. This is a new experience, and in retrospect was a dramatic harbinger that the trajectory of life had changed irreversibly. It was certainly going to be different to what I may have imagined.

I was excited, and my presence on the aircraft was evidence of my embarking on a new adventure. What follows is a highly personal – and therefore subjective – recollection of my time working for the Office of the United Nations High Commissioner for Refugees (which I refer to as "UNHCR"), mainly involved with the Vietnamese so-called "boat people". In the early days I wrote frequent letters home from Thailand, and fortunately my late father kept nearly all those I sent him. Extracts from these are scattered throughout the first part of the narrative, providing the naïve impressions of a much younger man as he wrestled with the challenges of the new and unknown.

· 1 ·

Geneva

When I graduated from Heriot Watt University in June 1974 with a BA Hons degree in Business Administration, my overriding desire was to get out of Scotland. My uncle Bill Fraser had suggested the practical option of going on to study to become qualified as a chartered accountant, but since I had found the accounting classes at university the least interesting of all the courses I had had to take, that direction offered no temptation.

At the time I was very keen on squash and had taken a qualification in basic coaching at the Edinburgh Sports Club from the late, great, Hadyn Davies, the manager of the club and an outstanding coach. I had imagined that in future it might enable me to earn extra money, and when I decided to go to study French overseas, I chose Geneva rather than any of the French universities because the university brochure advertised that there were squash courts in Geneva. By such weighty considerations are life paths set.

By February 1975, after a single semester of study at Geneva University in its "Cours de Langue et de Civilisation Francaise", I was running out of money and needed a job. By then I had a wonderful American girlfriend whom I had met at the University on the same course, and I wanted above all else to stay in the city. I thought that with a business degree I might be able to find a position at the GATT (the General

Agreement on Tariffs and Trade, which eventually became the World Trade Organisation).

So, appropriately equipped with a completed yellow P.11 UN application form I arranged a meeting with an official in the GATT headquarters, which was located on the shores of Lake Geneva in the Centre William Rappard. He told me there was nothing available at the time and asked if I had tried any of the other UN agencies. I had not. He therefore called a friend at UNHCR (the office of the UN High Commissioner for Refugees), to ask if there were any openings there. On being told there might be, he suggested that I should go over straight away.

I therefore walked up the road to the Palais des Nations clutching my application form, presented myself at the new extension building where UNHCR had its office on the 10th floor, with a splendid view over Lake Geneva and the Alps to the South. I was registered as a guest, took the lift up, and knocked at the door of Anita Tsitos (an Englishwoman married to a Greek), who was the Deputy Head of UNHCR Personnel. She was friendly, asked if I knew anything about book-keeping (which of course I claimed I did), we chatted a bit and, given that the UN is notoriously nepotistic and insular, then asked what was, probably, the key question:

"Do you know anyone who works for UNHCR?"

"No, but I know someone who used to work here, David Lambo."

"Ah, so you must be the young man David was talking about."

It so happened that in September 1974 I had travelled from the UK to Geneva by overnight train. On the train were two Nigerian brothers, David and Michael Lambo, who had been visiting London for their grandmother's funeral. It was a crowded, memorable and friendly journey of endless conversations during which none of us got any sleep, and in the morning Michael, the younger of the two brothers, got off the train in Lausanne where he was attending University.

The elder brother, David, continued to Geneva, and when we parted at the Gare Cornavin, he asked me to visit him at the Palais des Nations where he worked for the UNHCR. During my time at Geneva University, I visited him a couple of times for lunch at the Palais and learned something of the work that UNHCR was doing. He had subsequently moved to Kenya, and it turned out that he had been a close friend of Tsitos, and that he had mentioned my apparent interest in his work.

A further coincidence was that that very same morning, the Dane who had been the bookkeeper in the Public Information department of UNHCR had been promoted to a position in the finance department, so there was an immediate need for someone to keep the ledger for Public Information, a job that, at least on paper, I seemed qualified for. I was therefore hired on the spot on a 6-month contract and started work the next day.

That job only lasted for a few weeks however, and my struggles with the curious record-keeping system that my predecessor had introduced were brought to a premature but fortuitously rapid end by a new mission. After the fall of Saigon to Communist forces in April 1975, a large number of Vietnamese had fled the country, and some of them, sitting in evacuation centres in Guam and in the USA, had decided that they wanted to go home again. UNHCR had been asked to help their repatriation, the first stage of which was their completion of repatriation request forms, that UNHCR then had to "process" (which involved making four photocopies) and distribute to relevant parties such as the Vietnamese and US missions in Geneva.

I was asked to head up the repatriation (processing) team, which was given temporary accommodation in an office in the basement of the nearby ILO building, and which consisted of a very large photocopying machine, myself, and two part-time students from Africa who were studying at the University and who I hired on short-term contracts. Over the next few weeks, we churned out hundreds of forms and divided them into 4 or 5 piles, one of which we retained, while the others were sent to the different recipients. After several weeks, the flow of forms slowed, and then stopped altogether, since it became increasingly evident that the new Vietnamese regime had no interest in taking back anyone who had fled. I therefore had to let the two students go, and for most of the time sat reading in my basement retreat.

After a couple of weeks of this relaxed existence, I received a message that the High Commissioner's Executive Assistant wanted to see me. I made my way over to the head office and found Zia Rizvi holding a copy of a Private Eye article that I had photocopied and sent to a couple of friends in the office. The article was a sceptical report on the comfort and wealth of the former South Vietnamese leader, Nguyen Van Thieu, by that stage in exile in the USA. Rizvi asked me what I thought of the article and, seemingly satisfied by my response, asked what I was doing. I told him, in all honesty, not very much, whereupon he asked if I would like to go to Thailand.

The Thai Government had requested the UN's help to deal with the influx of refugees from (mainly) Laos who had started to cross the border in April at the end of the war and who, in reduced numbers, were still arriving. They were largely expecting to go back home, but as the political situation in Laos had not changed, they remained in limbo in Thailand. UNHCR was about to put together a package of assistance and needed more staff out there in a hurry. Did I want to go for 6 months? My initial reaction was that no, I didn't want to go. I had just started earning a reasonable salary (SFR 2,860 a month), I had just turned 24, shared a nice sunny studio flat with a lovely girlfriend, the skiing season was coming up; why would I want to go anywhere? Rizvi sensed my hesitation and asked me to think about it over the weekend (it was a Friday) and give him my answer on the following Monday.

By the Sunday night I had come to the conclusion that it was clearly an opportunity not to be missed, and so reported in on the Monday morning. Rizvi met me brusquely, immediately started talking about my mission "to Vientiane" (which was the capital of Laos – or by that stage, the People's Democratic Republic of Laos). I was able to correct him: that he had first suggested, and that I had agreed to, Thailand ("Well, you'd be just across the river").

He then started talking about a new position they were creating, that of Field Officers, who were to be based in the provinces close to the refugee areas, rather than in the capital city of the country. And my destination was to be the Northeast of Thailand. "When can you leave?" I was given time for a quick trip back to Scotland, and with promises to the girlfriend to reunite soon, was ready to go.

Three Field Officers were appointed initially. The only one with any relevant experience was Jacques Mouchet, a modest and thoughtful Savoyard who had previously lived and worked in Laos with UNHCR, spoke the Lao language, was married to a Laotian woman and had two children.

The other neophyte was David Jamieson, an ebullient and confident Briton with whom I would share many off-duty escapades. His father, Thomas Jamieson, who had died the year before, had been UNHCR's Director of Operations from

Jacques Mouchet   *David Jamieson*

1959 to 1972. (A Glaswegian, he was a pioneering figure in
the early days of refugee assistance, having also been chief of
operations of the UN Korean Reconstruction Agency after the
war there, as well as Director of Operations of UNRWA, the UN
Relief and Works Agency for Palestinian refugees.)

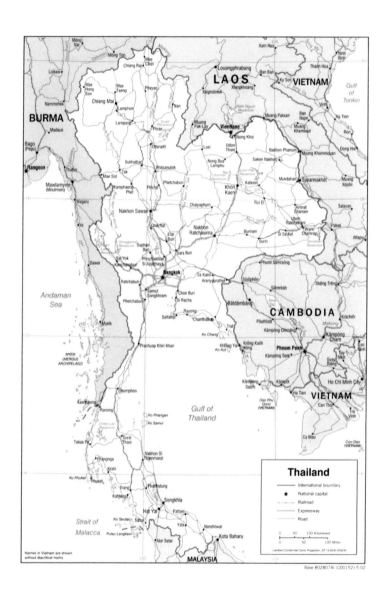

Thailand

— International boundary
★ National capital
— Railroad
— Expressway
— Road

0   50   100 Kilometers
0   50   100 Miles

Lambert Conformal Conic Projection, SP 12 60 N 39 60 N

Names in Vietnam are shown
without diacritical marks

Base 802807AI (C00152) 5-02

To Thailand and the Northeast

Mouchet had gone on ahead, so Jamieson and I agreed to travel out together. I had heard great things about a relatively new airline called Singapore Airlines and therefore asked the UN travel agent to book seats on it, which meant going to Rome to connect with the flight to Bangkok, with a refuelling stop in Bahrain. It was indeed a great service, and all went well until we had taken off from Bahrain when, as revealed earlier, the outer starboard engine burst into flames. We circled a few times to dump fuel and flew back to Bahrain for repairs. We disembarked, only to be told a couple of hours later that the engine could not be repaired, and that it would take 24 hours for a new engine to be sent from Singapore.

It was a Friday, Bahrain was closed, and the terminal had certainly not been designed for anything other than brief stopovers for international flights. There was minimal catering, barely any air conditioning, nowhere to lie down, and a full jumbo jet load of passengers getting increasingly sweaty, hungry, thirsty and bad-tempered. A stale sandwich was provided at some stage, but the single lift up to the restaurant broke down with a group of us inside, only saved from asphyxiation by a large Australian woman at the front who wrestled open the doors and we could climb out.

After a sleepless night on the floor, at last a replacement aircraft flew in and we could leave. As there were only 5 passengers scheduled to get off in Bangkok, the pilot decided to fly straight to Singapore, and on arrival there Jamieson and I were put on a connecting flight to Bangkok. When we finally disembarked it was around midday, and we had been travelling for nearly 48 hours. As we waited in the non-airconditioned baggage hall for our suitcases, the humidity and heat became more intense, and I became increasingly sweaty and irritable. The baggage hall consisted of a shed open to the elements, in which two circular carousels were hand-loaded from a trailer that pulled up outside.

The airport at Don Muang was also then the main base of the Royal Thai Air Force, the civilian terminal perched on the west side alongside the main road from Bangkok to the north. Bags safely retrieved, we hailed the first cab waiting outside and headed into town. In those days, the road to the airport still had klongs (canals) running along each side of it, and as we drove along, a buffalo hauled itself out of the water on our left, and there were still a few rice paddy fields along the highway, although they were soon to disappear. The dual carriageway ended abruptly at the outskirts of the city, and we were then engulfed in what was to become a recurrent and notorious feature of visits to the city, the traffic.

The High Commissioner himself, Sadruddin Aga Khan,[1]

---

1. Prince Sadruddin Aga Khan was a man of wealth, style, and substance. Perhaps, a more effective head of the UNHCR than any of the series of retired politicians and bureaucrats who succeeded him. In the words of the Guardian obituary, *"His mother was French, his father had lived his early life in India but was of Iranian descent and had acquired British nationality. Sadruddin saw himself as a citizen of the world - a multilingual, highly cultured cosmopolitan, familiar with the upper echelons of international society, who nevertheless became passionately involved with the plight of successive and growing waves of refugees and the seemingly insoluble problems of resettlement....He was a good man who believed in the duty of elites to improve the lot of humanity."* He also thought he should be the UN Secretary General but failed in two attempts to be elected.

had by this time arrived in the country for an official visit to the Thai Government, and so we were booked into the same hotel as the main entourage (the old Erewan Hotel, an elegant two storey building at the corner of Ratchdamri and Ploenchit roads. (Sadly, its very central location meant that it was demolished a few years later, and the site is now occupied by the garish Grand Hyatt Erewan Hotel). Here we stayed in great comfort for a week with not much work to do except appear at official events as required and visit the nearby office which was then located in an apartment building opposite the British Embassy.

The first day we went to the office the local staff took us out for lunch at a food stall on the street, warning us about the dangers of the very hot local chili peppers, the "priki-noo". In a moment of temporary insanity, David boasted of his ability to eat them raw. We all watched, transfixed, as he bit down. He began to turn red, then even redder; his eyes started streaming; beads of sweat began to break out on his forehead and ran down his cheeks. He grabbed and downed a glass of water, which clearly made the burning worse, and finally the laughing stall owner handed him a banana to eat, which seemed to relieve the burning. It was a valuable and, for him, a painful way to learn a key lesson in local survival skills. (I subsequently found out that wrapping a priki-noo in omelette completely killed its heat).

We did manage to explore the city a bit in that first week, initially being waylaid outside the hotel by one of the many taxi drivers who lurked in wait for naïve visitors. We fell for his sales pitch once, and were taken on the inevitable tour of tacky tourist shops and a particularly grim massage parlour that put us off the idea of repeating it, at least for a while. Another day we hired a long-tailed boat to explore some of the canals, and once out of the sight and sound of road traffic, it was like stepping back into time, watching people who lived on their boats and worked up and down the river and canal system. But this seductive image of any notion of a timeless and unspoilt way of life was shattered when we passed a boat in which a young mother was crying hysterically – the guide said that she had just lost her baby who had been sleeping in a hammock strung at the back of the boat, now swinging emptily.

After the week of official receptions and unaccustomed luxury, David left for Aranyaprathet on the Cambodian border, and I departed for the Northeast accompanied by a Swiss UNHCR colleague, Werner Blatter, who had previously served in the Vientiane office and spoke a bit of Lao. As we flew into Udorn Thani airport (the civilian section of which occupied a small part of a very large US/Thai airbase) in the twin propellor-driven de Havilland Avro 748 of Thai Airways, three F-4 Phantom jets of the US Air Force took off in the opposite direction.[2]

The civilian terminal was tucked away in a remote corner of the airbase, and to get out of the airport we had to hire a local taxi, get past first American, then Thai, military security.

Having driven past a row of seedy bars and massage parlours outside the base (one appealingly called "Magic Fingers") we arrived in Udorn town centre and drove to a hotel. Werner thought the first thing we should do was to pay a visit to the Governor of the province. We therefore hired another taxi and turned up at the Salakarn Changwat (the provincial office) and

---

2. In the 1960's the Thai Government allowed the US to build a number of airbases in the country as a countermeasure to the growing Vietnamese -driven Communist insurgency in Laos and the North East of Thailand which it feared might spread further into the country. These bases were used with increasing intensity as the Vietnam war progressed, and around each one a basic service economy developed.

were ushered into the office of a clearly bewildered Governor, who had never previously had to receive a delegation from the UNHCR. He could not speak English, knew nothing of the supposed assistance programme that had just been agreed in Bangkok, and said that there were no refugees in the province, and that we might find some in Nong Khai province, some 60 kms to the north.

Diplomatic courtesies completed, we also paid a courtesy call on the US Consulate in Udorn. Of course, the Americans knew all about our visit and the programme and were very helpful. They were keen to find out as much as they could about the situation in Laos and thought that the Lao community that had fled into Thailand could be a useful source of information.

The following morning, having negotiated a price with the driver of the taxi that we judged had the best chance of completing the trip, we set out for Nong Khai situated on the banks of the mighty Mekong River. First stop in Nong Khai was, of course, the Salakarn Changwat, to meet a similar monolingual Governor. He acknowledged the presence of a large number of Laotians in his province, most of them housed in rented accommodation (their funds had not yet run out and most were hoping to return home). We explained the plan to provide funds, through the Ministry of Interior in Bangkok, to help house, feed, and possibly resettle them in other countries, at which point he became much more interested.

The interview ended, we went to what appeared to be the smartest hotel in town and almost immediately Werner bumped into people he had known in Vientiane. Word that the UN had arrived spread fast, and soon large numbers of people came by the hotel to see Werner and to find out what was going on.

The immediate answer was – very little. The UN had to

The Mekong at sunset

request funds for new programmes from its donors, and this process was still under way, so the first of the promised funds had yet to be sent to Bangkok, and the Ministry of the Interior had not yet received any budgets from the provinces that hosted the refugee populations. All that would take time to arrange. That evening, I took Werner to the station for his overnight train back to Bangkok, his parting words to me being: "Give us a call sometime". That was about the sum total of my briefing.[3]

---

3. In fairness, before leaving Geneva, I had been summoned to meet one of the directors, a Belgian, Gilbert Jaeger, who had no doubt been involved in the decision to approve my mission. He had never been to Thailand, so wasn't able to offer much advice, but did tell me that I should always remember that I represented the UN, and that if I ever had to roll my sleeves up and do dirty work, I should do so "with dignity".

Earlier in the day, we had already made a call to the Bangkok office, which entailed a visit to the "*Choomsai Torasap*", the telephone exchange, where we had had to book a call, and then wait for 35 minutes for it to go through. I could already see that communications with the regional office would not be regular, nor could they be urgent. It subsequently turned out that the waiting time would range from 5 minutes (exceptionally) to never (when the call couldn't go through); the average time being between 25-60 minutes. While this technical hurdle was initially rather disturbing as I had no means of quickly asking advice from more senior colleagues, in fact over time it became a useful means of justifying any decision or action that I took.

The days that followed were a blur. I had no idea what I was doing but, little by little, heard many haunting personal stories, learned a lot about recent history, discovered that there were some refugees who had family overseas (mainly in France), and that while some of them wanted to go there, most just wanted to go back home once things had settled down in Laos. There were occasional visits to the local Government officers to help them start to put budgets together, although language difficulties prevented much meaningful dialogue.

The first night I went out to a restaurant, where I was the only foreigner. None of the staff spoke English. I used sign language to ask for a menu, but this too was written entirely in Thai. With some embarrassment, by pointing to what other people in the restaurant were eating and drinking, I managed to order a plate of fried rice and a beer. I decided then and there that I would have to learn enough Thai to be able to order food, read road signs, and tell a taxi driver where I wanted to go. As soon as I got back to Bangkok I bought a copy of a book entitled "The Fundamentals of the Thai Language", which I worked through from cover to cover at least three times, and

it became my lifeline and insight into the very different world
I had entered.

My presence in the town meant that I had an endless
stream of Laotian visitors, all anxious to share rumours that
they had heard, to find out what the international community
was doing about Laos (they assumed, wrongly, that something
was being done, and that the UN would have an inside track
on any information), or when they would be allowed to go
home, or travel overseas to stay with their relatives. Most still
had funds and were renting accommodation in Nong Khai,
and as many could speak French, communications were
relatively easy. I fortuitously discovered a small Vietnamese
bakery and restaurant which made excellent croissants, bread,
and delicious spring rolls, and became a regular customer.

In the evening the shops and restaurants closed early and
the town fell silent, broken occasionally by the barking of
dogs or the sound of gunfire from across the river in Laos. I
would sometimes wander through the darkened streets and
recall one evening as I was passing a house closed up behind
a high fence, from out of an upstairs window the strains of an
aria from the Marriage of Figaro rang out. I stopped to listen,
gripped by the unexpected magic spell. It didn't last long, and
when it ended I was pitched back into the enveloping warmth
of the tropical night.

After a few futile weeks of repeating to the Laotians that
nothing was happening in the assistance programme that had
been announced, I returned to Bangkok to await its 'implementation' (a notorious, oft-used word in UN parlance), taking
time to talk with the resettlement staff, pick up registration
forms, learn more about the wider issues, and take my frustrations out on my superiors, who seemed to me to be too
supine in the face of the bureaucratic delays at HQ and within
the Thai Government. They clearly disagreed, and I developed

a doubtless well-earned reputation for being a little hot-headed. One particular incident was provoked by the Deputy Representative saying that the UN in Thailand should be prepared to "lose face", to which I had counter-argued, perhaps a little too forcefully, that in my view the UN in Thailand was there to get things done.

Letter home dated 12 November 1975

"The refugees are divided between three main areas (i) the Southeast of Thailand, around the Cambodian border where the Khmer stay (ii) the Northeastern provinces centred around Nong Khai and Nam Phong, where there are over 20,00 Hmong and Lao and (iii) further to the north, near Chiang Mai, where there are undetermined numbers of Hmong and Yao (another hilltribe). Precise numbers are hard to assess because more arrive each day – 57 crossed the Mekong at Nong Khai yesterday. The Pathet Lao occasionally fire at fleeing people; 6 were killed last week when a rocket-propelled grenade landed in their boat. In the river district of Nong Khai there has been a build-up of military equipment, and from time to time, PL soldiers loose off automatic rifle fire at the opposite shore. Thus far there has been only one fatality, but damage has been done to various buildings including the station… Meanwhile the ferries still ply between the two countries, occasionally halted by unilateral closing of the border by either side, usually in turns, and Laotians still come to shop in NongKhai.

"We have field offices in each of the main areas and we are about to be reinforced … because UNHCR headquarters had received reports (mainly from the US Embassy, which had told us nothing) that the UN programme was not being

properly organised. HQ had read exaggerated reports of camp conditions and mortality rates, and so sent us a cable demanding an explanation. It also said that it had had reports of large groups of refugees "uncovered" by field staff. Again, the work of the USA, and again, untrue.

"HQ's initial reaction to the refugees from Laos was one of the more disgraceful policies they have followed recently. It decided initially to ignore the Lao refugees in Thailand …since they already had an assistance programme within Laos and were embarrassed by having two policies towards the Lao in two different countries. Thus, no help for re-settlement, largely because many were considered to be "economic" refugees.

"After only about 6 weeks here, I refused to come back to the area until, or unless, the policy was changed. A cable was sent to HQ explaining (and perhaps slightly exaggerating) the situation with the refugees. It had even got to the stage whereby a group of about 150 Thai Dam knew they had been granted visas by France, and also knew that UNHCR was blocking their movement."

A major issue was the fact that the bulk of the funds promised to the Thai Government for the programme was still being raised and the first tranche was slow in being transferred to the Ministry of Interior in Bangkok, which meant that nothing could be sent to the provinces where it was needed. After exchanges of cables from the Bangkok office, Geneva relented, and confirmed both the change in policy to enable resettlement and, more importantly, a transfer of funds.

In response to the pressure from the US to get more staff into the field, I was joined at the beginning of November by a second field officer in the form of a young French

Gregoire de Brancovan

national, Gregoire de Brancovan,[4] whose family knew the High Commissioner.

I duly returned to the field with Gregoire, and since the resettlement programme for the Lao refugees had finally begun to pick up in earnest, we had to be in the camp on a daily basis and so decided to stay in Nong Khai. We initially stayed in an unheated hotel on the outskirts of town for a few (bitterly cold) weeks, and then rented a house close to the river. This provided basic living with, of course, no air conditioning or

---

4. I subsequently found out some years later that Gregoire was, in fact, Prince Gregoire Bessaraba de Brancovan, a scion of an ancient Moldavian dynasty that had given its name to Bessarabia in modern day Romania, and which had apparently reigned over the Danubian principality of Walachia, a vassal state of the Ottoman Turks, from 1601. He married a Laotian of Thai Dam origin and spent his career in UNHCR. I caught up with him again in 2019 in Paris, where he was living by himself in his spacious apartment, his wife away in New York. It was the last time I saw him, as he died the following year.

hot water, abundant mosquitoes and countless other insects, with prickly heat a regular irritation.

Letter home 23 April 1976

"A wooden building with a distinct lack of luxury, the house contains two small bedrooms, a large open living area, a bathroom with a shower but no water pressure whatsoever, BUT with a "European style toilet". There is a space downstairs which is much cooler but totally uninhabitable because of the mosquitos .. an added hazard is that during the rainy season, about to break on us with full fury, the lower portion of the house is flooded, due to the proximity of the Mekong River which has a tendency to break its banks from time to time…at this precise moment you find me sitting under two electric fans, pausing in typing rhythm only to swat the over-active mosquitos which attack my ankles despite having one fan at ground level to prevent exactly that."

We hired Samlee, a lazy but good-natured young local girl as housekeeper, who stirred occasionally to make feeble attempts to keep the house from being overwhelmed by dust, occasionally cooked basic food, and whose main initiative in the time we were there was to sell the mangoes from the large tree in the garden. We had been anticipating a huge harvest of ripe mangos, but upon return from a routine trip to Bangkok, found that the tree had been stripped bare, unaware that in the Northeast mangos tend to be eaten unripe, chopped up into one of the staple – and delicious – local dishes, *Som Tam*, or *Tam Muk Muang*.

Eventually we decided that staying out of the immediate reach of the refugees would be more prudent, so Gregoire and I each rented a house in Udorn. Mine was not far from the US

Nong Prachak at dusk

Consulate beside the Nong Prachak pond, and I subsequently became very good friends with the vice consul, Mason "Hank" Hendrickson, who became my tennis, golf and drinking partner. In the dying days of the US presence, Udorn was very much a frontier town, hot and dusty in the daytime, brooding and restless at night.

The airbase had provided a temporary boom to the local economy, but after the Thai Government had asked the US to withdraw from Thailand at the end of 1975, the bases closed down and all the American personnel were pulled out. Despite rumours that the Americans would return, Udorn slipped back into its former rural insignificance. The service economy that had grown up around the bases faded away, but it meant however that for a while, wherever we went, as Westerners we were guaranteed enthusiastic service, living symbols of past good times and vanishing prosperity.

The office procured a second hand Landrover which I was

instructed to have painted white with large UNHCR letters in blue on the side and the roof to make it obvious to any CT's (communist terrorists) that we were nothing to do with the government, since at the time they were reported to be active in 32 of Thailand's 74 provinces, including most of the northeast.

Letter home 10 February 1976

"We obtained a Landrover about a month ago which I was extremely content to drive around myself until Geneva insisted that I find a driver, and so the necessary steps have been taken. Meanwhile we have had to paint it white with big blue UNHCR letters on every side and on top, ostensibly to ward off any communist terrorists when we venture into more remote areas of the country, which is not all that infrequent.

"Tomorrow, I depart for Nakorn Phanom at crack of dawn to investigate a newspaper report that 500 refugees

had recently crossed over as a result of continued fighting in the south of Laos. It appears that one of the royal princes has decided to go back and lead a guerrilla movement, which adds to the substantial trouble the Hmong are still causing the Pathet Lao in the region north of Vientiane – bridges blown, convoys attacked, roads impassable. Reports suggest that the Hmong have 2-3 years supply of arms and munitions hidden in the hills, so the chances of a protracted guerilla struggle are high.

"The border here was closed for some weeks because of a much-publicised gunboat incident in which a Thai sailor was killed and a gunboat grounded by PL fire. However, it was opened again after a short period during which the Lao were reminded how much they depended on trade with Thailand, and now at least the NongKhai crossing is open.

"There are big protection problems at the moment, with some refugees being detained and charged as illegal aliens. Once they have passed a mandatory 25 days in gaol they are then technically supposed to be sent back to Laos. Up until now not many have been, but news filters out that the Governor is about to forcibly repatriate a large group, which won't go down well in Geneva regardless of the fact that the Thais can do exactly what they want to, not being signatories to the Protocol and Convention relating to the status of refugees.

"If a refugee has enough money, it is a completely different story, and little anguish is suffered. The Thais are paid off (Baht 4,000 to immigration officials to get in, around Baht 1,300 to the police to get out of gaol, and around Baht 600 to the camp authorities to be allowed into the camp) and life thereafter is reasonably secure."

In my white UN-labelled Landrover I would take occasional

long unaccompanied trips to other towns along the Mekong River to follow up on reports of refugee arrivals or detentions, to Sri Chieng Mai, Bueng Kan, Nakorn Phanom, and Mukdahan, all the way down to Ubon Ratchathani. In each province, since my presence would have been reported as soon as I had passed any of the military or police checkpoints along the road, I would call on the Governor's office to explain why I was there. There was little traffic on the (generally very good) roads, and the sense of complete freedom as I drove along under the flame trees that lined both sides of the highway was both inspiring and even a little overwhelming.

Usually there was nobody to find; most of the Lao had either gone home again, or were staying with relatives, or had no desire to be moved into the camp. At any rate, as suggested above, anyone who wanted to get into a camp, usually could. From time to time a family destined for resettlement would report a missing relative, and I recall one evening, accompanied by an official from the Nongkhai Salaklarng, I had to go to Sri Chieng Mai along the river to find a young girl whose family had been accepted for resettlement in France.

We found her place of work, a dingy bar frequented by armed off-duty military types who did not look amused when a young foreigner walked in. The girl was summoned, the official explained why we were there, and that she could go to France; but she said she was quite happy and had no desire to go anywhere. She didn't give the impression of being under coercion, and the official later said she had become the mistress of one of the army officers. So we left her there. It wasn't clear how, or even whether, she was related to the family, who didn't seem too surprised or upset at the thought that she wanted to stay behind.

One of the underlying problems that we had to bear in mind was that, as I had mentioned in one of my letters, Thailand,

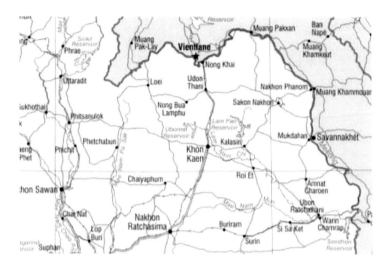

like all the countries in the region, had never signed the
International Protocol and Convention relating to the status of
refugees and were therefore under no obligation to adhere to
its guidelines and could at any time have sent all of them back.
Some groups either volunteered or were encouraged to return,
with grim stories emerging about treatment of the few who
went back to Cambodia.

Letter home 10 February 1976
*"Cambodia has recently reopened diplomatic relations
with Thailand and says it wants all the refugees to return.
A group of around 70 Cambodians returned voluntarily
shortly after the fall of Phnom Penh – greeted with smiles at
the frontier, they were all executed 3 hours later. The exact
story of what happened in Cambodia (and is still happening) will probably never be fully told. It may be that up to
2-3 million have been butchered (out of a population of 7
million) ... some of the stories that the refugees arrive with
are unbelievable and make your hair stand on end ... even*

if exaggerated, they are chilling in the extreme. The veneer of civilisation is indeed thin."

When I had first agreed to go to Thailand, I had been given a six-month contract, mainly because nobody knew at the time how long the programme would last, and I had therefore anticipated that I would be returning to Geneva. The main reason for wanting to go back was really the beautiful Lisa, but as the end of the six months drew closer, and the work became more engaging and interesting, I began to have second thoughts, and at the same time Werner was advising me that I would be much better off staying in the field.

Letter home 10 February 1976
"Having been here 5 months now, I have decided to stay on until the end of the year for a variety of different reasons, not least the fact that the job is nowhere near being finished. Whether it will finish by the end of December remains to be seen, but given the political situation in the area, it seems highly doubtful... It makes more sense of the job and the responsibilities involved if I feel I can't just come for a brief experience and then leave again with everything still in disarray... Anyway, a message from Geneva said that there was no job for me there, so at least I am still employed.

"On reflection, I really don't want to go back and work in Geneva, much as though I like the town and life there, the thought of returning to that bureaucracy of bureaucracies and running a regular existence sends shivers up my spine. Doubtless I'll have to do it sooner or later, but as I have the choice of having a job with no defining limits, no office hours, a high degree of mobility and activity, the decision wasn't a hard one."

Once I had decided to stay on, prompted by the note from Headquarters stating that I would not have a job there, I suggested to Lisa that she come out to join me to which, after some hesitation, she agreed. She had come out for a 10-day holiday in December, and while it had been awkward for the first few days, by the time she left it felt that we were back in tune again and looking forward to the future. But as the time approached, I was becoming increasingly absorbed and busier in the work, and eventually got cold feet and suggested that she should not come after all. It was perhaps an ignoble conclusion, but an honest one, since at the time I was barely able to handle the various personal and professional challenges and I didn't think I could face the ties and added responsibility of taking care of someone else as well. So ended what had been a short, but intense, rich, and fulfilling relationship.

Letter home 23 April 1976

"The work is still interesting, rewarding, challenging, and I am still very happy doing it. The longer I stay in Thailand, the more I begin to appreciate the opportunity of being in the East. I feel a rate of change in me that is very rapid.

"We have just had a visit from two French officials, one from the Bangkok embassy, the other from Paris. France has now decided to resettle all the Thai Dam and Thai Nung in various agricultural region of France, so the visit was primarily to arrange the first group for departure... So yet more friends who will soon be leaving. In many ways it's a strange job, particularly in terms of the relationships one has with the refugees.

"Amongst the thousands that one meets or works with, there are only very few with whom any sort of close rapport is possible. These never stay long, departing to new and difficult lives abroad, and each time the buses leave the camp

early on Sunday mornings, they always take with them someone who has come to mean more than the rest. Hence a persistent awareness of how transitory relationships are, and how important it should be to recognise something of value when it presents itself. I feel I'm learning slowly and that has to be a good tendency if it means appreciating events as they happen and, especially, people as they appear, and not later when it's too late to be of any worth."

"We recently had to entertain a big chief from Austcare, a big Australian voluntary agency, who was supposed to be high-powered, had much influence etc. Therefore, great expectations were set. She turned out to be American, had no idea about what was going on here, had practically no experience with refugees, and seemed more content to have herself photographed with Thai Dam girls in traditional dress than to ask any really pertinent questions. The crowning glory was when she asked the group of girls what they thought of women's liberation ... to see the five exquisitely dressed and sublimely feminine girls next to the blue-jean clad visitor provided a contrast will linger long in the memory."

But fortunately, not all the visitors we had to entertain were so self-interested and myopic. Many were genuinely interested and sincere.

"We also had a visit from a couple of Danes, one a psychology lecturer and President of the Danish Refugee Council, the other a member of the Ministry of Foreign Affairs who sits on the UNHCR Executive Committee. Both were very interested in conditions and what was going on, and both made a real effort to try and understand all the problems involved in this particular area. The Hmong part of the

camp filled both with horror, which brought to mind my own initial impressions of the camps, and also reinforced the notions I've recently had about how quickly one becomes accustomed to any situation. To be asked questions that hadn't been posed for a long time made me think harder about what I live with and forced me to find answers. Their reactions were obviously naively direct and for that reason provoked more thought than usual. In all a very refreshing time and a delight to be able to communicate with two intelligent and genuine people."

"Am due back in Bangkok next week, after a stop in Ubol, close to the Thai border on the eastern frontier. Refugee problems in that area do not take on the same proportions, and relations with the authorities are much better than up here, greater co-operation being the name of the game. I always enjoy going to Ubol and staying in what must be one of the best hotels in Thailand outside Bangkok … of course all built with American money in the days of their military presence. Ubol was one of the biggest air bases and was used for raids into the Central Highlands of Vietnam and into Cambodia."

This trip was the result of the delivery of a battered Peugot 504 which had been used by the UNHCR office in Vientiane, which I was asked to take down to Bangkok. I jumped at the chance of being on my own again, left the Landrover and driver with Gregoire, and headed southeast one morning across the Isan plateau through Kalasin and Yasothorn, to Ubon. I visited the camp there, where I was (as usual) handed various hand-written notes from the inhabitants, most of them rather desperate and touching.

This was a typical offering, dated 5-8-76:

"To Sir with respect.

"First I must apologise to write a letter. I know well I bother you to help me and my wife. Because I'm crazy about going to Australia. Sir, I'm an orphant (sic) and become destitute from Lao communist and I don't know how to fine (sic) the benefactor.

"Sir, I don't know how to write English very well. Please forgive me and pity me. Because I do want to know English very well and improve it. I do know I'm late for the old project for Australia and America, and I don't know how long will they have the new project, sir, I feel hurt about my improving English. I'm an English teacher as I told you when you were visiting Lao camp Ubol I had taught English about six years before Lao communist overpowered and then I stopped teaching.

"Even I'm 27 years old, and I'm feeble minded about speaking and writing. However, I do hope you will answer me. Please and please help me. Sir, I and my wife want to see the prosper country and to be pleasant to look at. And the most important of my English I surely say I do need Australia system. Oh! Please God help me. Even if I don't know you but I must think of your kindness and benevolent.

"End of this. I don't know how to thank you. Well I take this opportunity to wish you, say God take care of you and your family and all your hope can be done easily and smoothly.

"Sincerely yours, from Lao refugee Phommavady".

I would receive hundreds of similar notes over the years, even though there was little or nothing I could do to help on a personal basis. The chances of any of the refugees being reset-tled depended largely on whether they had relatives abroad. The main accepting countries (the USA and France initially)

would announce limited resettlement projects, aimed primarily at family reunion. Sometimes the qualifying criteria were expanded to include people with specific credentials, but numbers were always limited. I do not recall what happened to Phommavady.

The UN's role in the resettlement process was important, but in fact extremely limited, and while we could occasionally draw the attention of the immigration teams to well qualified applicants, we had no influence at all over their decisions. For the refugees we represented hope, but it just wasn't possible to either act on or reply to most of the notes that were passed on.

After a couple of nights there, I set off again along the northern Cambodian border to check whether there were any Cambodian refugees who had managed to escape across the hills. At the time there were almost no visitors to the area due to the fairly frequent armed clashes between the Khmer Rouge and the Thai army, particularly around the area of the Khao Preah Vihear complex, an old Khmer temple perched on

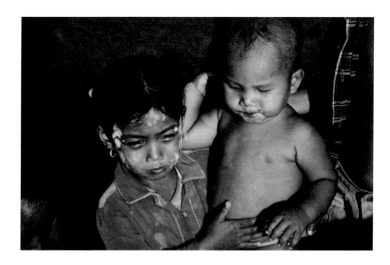

the top of the Dangrek mountain range that marks the frontier between Thailand and Cambodia.

The whole area to the north of the mountains used to be part of the ancient empire ruled by the Khmer kings of Angkor, as many ancient temple structures in the Khmer style bear witness. The only Cambodian I came across was a captured Khmer Rouge soldier, still in his black pyjama uniform, who was being held in a caged area at the back of the police station in Sisaket, where he was engaged in making a pair of rubber sandals from a car tyre – with his teeth.

I based myself for a couple of nights in the next provincial capital, Surin, another seemingly moribund town that at night was dark, empty and slightly sinister. At a restaurant close to the hotel, I got to know the only other Khmer I met on the trip, an attractive waitress from whom I learned that around 30% of the local Thai population of the province at the time were, in fact, ethnically Khmer, some of whom probably had relatives living in Cambodia. This may have partly explained why there appeared to be no pockets of destitute refugees to

be found in that area, but the mountain range that separates the two countries is very steep on the Cambodian side, was covered in jungle, and presented a formidable natural barrier for anyone trying to cross, let alone someone who had been able to hide from the pitiless Khmer Rouge guards.

Ban Vinai and the Hmong

When the Vietnam war ended in April 1975, the communist Pathet Lao, which by that stage already controlled most of the country, took over Vientiane and the rest of Laos, resulting in the flight across the Mekong river of thousands of Lao civilians (some of whom ended up in Nong Khai), as well as the CIA-backed and financed Hmong army led by General Vang Pao, who because they had done most of the bitter fighting marked by atrocities on both sides, were particularly targeted by the North Vietnamese and Pathet Lao.

An armistice in 1973 had been signed between the Pathet Lao and the Royal Lao Army, (the first time in history, as an observer quipped at the time, that an armistice had been signed between non-combatants) while the actual fighting was mainly between the Hmong and North Vietnamese regulars. In May 1975, the Hmong leadership and several thousand followers were airlifted from the CIA base in Long Cheng in Laos, and taken to the Royal Thai Air Base at Nam Pong in Khon Kaen province, which from 1972 had become a base of operations for the US Marine Corps.

The rest of the Hmong fighters and their families were told to try to get to Thailand as best they could. Many thousands eventually crossed over into the northern provinces of Chiang Rai, Phayao, Uttaradit, Nan, and Phitsanulok, often attacked and harassed by the Vietnamese army as they left. In the Nong Khai camp I came across a woman who had had to flee with her family while in an advanced state of pregnancy. She gave

birth on the trail, apparently rested for a few hours, and then continued on to the border. The child survived.

From Nam Pong, Vang Pao and his immediate entourage were flown out to be resettled in the USA, and the UN was not given access to the camp until it was agreed by the Thais and the Americans that the remaining population should also all be resettled. I was therefore the first person from the UN to be allowed into the camp, entry to which necessitated having to pass through several military checkpoints. There, I met Dr. Yang Dao,[5] an extremely intelligent and seductively articulate former adviser to Vang Pao.

The Thai army then decided to move the entire camp

---

5. Yang Dao told me that when the war in Laos started, he was at the top of his class and was sent to France to complete his education. After high school, he received one scholarship to study at the University of Paris, then another to study at the Sorbonne, and in May 1972 became the first Hmong to receive a PhD (in social and economic development). He returned to Laos despite the war, but three years later in May 1975 the ceasefire between the Pathet Lao

population to a new camp it constructed (with American money) at Ban Vinai, Pak Chom in Loei province, a site (not co-incidentally) selected close to one of the areas where Thai communists had been based after the 1973 coup d'etat, and astride one of the main infiltration routes from Laos.

Once the camp was occupied, UNHCR was expected to be involved in the resettlement process (at least for those who would not otherwise be sent to the USA). But since the road between Nong Khai and Pak Chom along the river was not secure, initially to get to the camp we had had to go on a long detour to the south.

One time when a senior delegation of UNHCR directors from Geneva visited the camps, we were flown over from Udorn in army helicopters, which made a show of climbing up to a great height over the hills, supposedly to be out of range of any ground-to-air fire. Whether or not there was any genuine threat was, fortunately, not tested. Eventually the unpaved riverside road was re-opened, but only for travel during day-light hours.

---

and the Royal Lao Army had broken down, and the North Vietnamese had surrounded Long Cheng where General Vang Pao and his army were based. He travelled there to meet the general who finally agreed to leave the country under pressure from the Americans, who flew him out to Nam Phong. Yang Dao subsequently left for Thailand with his family, crossing the Mekong by night and making his way to the camp. They were later resettled in France.

· 3 ·

The Political Backdrop

The Field Officers inevitably had to deal on a regular basis with the numerous officials in the border provinces where the camps were located. These included District Officers, local police, Provincial Governors, the paramilitary Border Patrol Police (BBP), and Army officers. Many border provinces were effectively under martial rule at the time, and roadblocks manned by the BPP, by soldiers or by police were widespread, especially between provinces and on the roads nearest to the border. Interactions and relationships with these groups became gradually more relaxed as they got used to our presence, and as we learned to navigate around them.

If we thought our life upcountry was tricky, it was relatively straightforward compared to what our colleagues in Bangkok had to deal with. The official counterparty was the Ministry of Interior, a bureaucracy of Byzantine complexity and which usually provided one or two officials with excellent English to deal with us. But its decision-making process was always concealed behind a mask of polite obfuscation. Since the refugees were regarded as a security threat, we also had to deal with the Internal Security Operations Command (ISOC) which was part of the Office of the Prime Minister. ISOC was also responsible for intelligence matters, staffed by intelligent hard-liners who generally looked on the UN as an annoyance or *agent provocateur*.

Behind the civilian apparatus of government lay the military, which since the 1932 revolution that had overthrown the absolute monarchy and had started the transition of the country into a constitutional monarchy and fledgling democracy, had seen itself as the bulwark of traditional values and guardian of the Thai nation. The revolution, in effect a military coup d'etat, had been driven by economic troubles, incompetent government, and the emergence of a Western-educated elite keen to modernise the country's political structure. While the change of power was largely bloodless, there were many disagreements over the path to be followed, resulting in two further coups d'etat the following year.

Each time anything like a democratic administration was established, it soon broke down in in-fighting, and the military stepped in to maintain order (and its power). By the time UNHCR set up office in 1975, there had been 11 further rebellions or coup d'etats, and in 1976 we were witness to yet another. At the time Thailand had been under civilian rule for only three years, after the overthrow in 1973 of the then Prime Minister Thanom Kittikachorn, a former Supreme Commander of the Thai Armed Forces who had assumed power in 1963 after the death of his former chief Sarit Thanarat, a legendary figure among Thailand's many military dictators (largely on account of his rumoured 100 mistresses, to each of whom he was reputed to have given a house and a Mercedes Benz).

Thanom had staged a coup against his own government in 1971, dissolving parliament on the pretext that it was necessary to defend the nation from the threat of Communism, but growing public discontent led by students led to three days of violence and the collapse of the regime. He went into voluntary exile which led to the restoration of a fragile democratic rule, but in 1976 he returned to Thailand as a monk, which provoked further student unrest focussed at Thammasat

University.[6] A year earlier, Vietnam, Laos and Cambodia had all fallen to the Communists, and the Thai military were paranoid that Thailand might share a similar fate, especially since the US bases in the country had been closed (by the civilian administration) at the end of 1975.

Following a couple of earlier provocations in which people had been killed, on 6 October 1976, right-wing militants and government security forces stormed the Thammasat campus, crushed the protests with shocking brutality and many students were killed. The military seized power again and installed a hard-line royalist as Prime Minister. But it was short-lived; a year later another bloodless military coup took place, with the then Supreme Commander General Kriangsak Chamanan being appointed Prime Minister. He turned out to be an effective leader and stayed in the post until he retired in 1980.

In the space of two years therefore, we had been witness to two coups d'etat, and had had to deal with three different Prime Ministers and their attendant changes in ministerial appointments. This naturally had a directly negative impact on the ability to communicate with the Government. The effects of all this rippled out to the provinces but in fact made little difference to our interaction with local officials.

The coups were always announced with the suspension of normal radio and TV programmes, replaced by martial music. They were also usually accompanied by a bout of paternalistic moralising, which entailed the imposition of night-time curfews, restrictions on the opening hours of entertainment

6. Thanom kept a low profile after he came out of the monkhood, and lived until 2004, with the Thai Queen presiding over his royally-sponsored cremation ceremony in 2007. I was to meet him occasionally at family events in the 1990's, a distinguished figure who retained great charisma, since my then father-in-law was his cousin.

places, and other annoyances such as increased roadblocks to catch curfew breakers or more traffic offenders than usual. Fortunately, these social constraints never lasted long, and the habitual Thai "*mai ben rai*" (never mind/don't worry/it doesn't matter) attitude would reassert itself.

Democracy as exercised in Thailand was – and seemingly still is – regarded by some as an indulgence. The original overthrow of the absolute monarchy was merely the replacement of a single source of authority by a wider coalition of the country's elite. Their attitude towards the population could be called one of benevolent despotism, which increasingly angered the growing minority of overseas educated people who demanded greater representation (on behalf of the people, of course). Any democratic administration was quickly engulfed in corruption, in-fighting, greed, incompetence, and favouritism, indeed the same qualities that marked every military government. It was more a question of who controlled the spoils.

When things got out of hand again, either the people would be on the streets demanding the overthrow of tyranny, or the military would step in to overthrow the civilian-engendered chaos that it would claim was a threat to the nation. In both cases, and increasingly so as the monarch aged and the old guard of military strongmen left the scene, the king would have to step in and remind his wayward subjects that they should behave better, and calm would be restored until the cycle began again.

4

To the South

When I got back to Bangkok after my trip to Ubol and Surin, I was informed that I was to be transferred to the South. I was reluctant to leave the Northeast, for despite it being the poorest and least geographically attractive region of Thailand, there was something about it that had resonated deeply with me. I had visited temples, attended festivals, and had read a lot about the history of the region and about the local Buddhist culture which was imbued with ancient spirit cults and animistic influences. Also, I felt that after a year in the field, I had only just begun to be more effective as a field operative.

But refugees from Vietnam had started to arrive in boats along the coast of the Gulf of Thailand in the southern part of the country and had then been transferred to a makeshift camp on vacant land opposite the police headquarters building in Songkhla. These were the first of the "boat people" who were to become a focus of international media attention.

While the Thais had little or no enthusiasm about refugees crossing into Thailand, the Vietnamese boat people, in particular, were not at all welcome. In large part this stemmed from the historic rivalry between Vietnam and Siam, and while there were small communities of Vietnamese in Thailand, mainly in and around Bangkok and in the Northeast where some Vietnamese had settled in 1954 after the communist takeover of North Vietnam. But they were distrusted, and

indeed, shortly after my arrival in Nongkhai in 1975, anti-Vietnamese riots occurred in which several shop-houses and residences of Vietnamese settlers were burned and looted (although, fortunately, not my favourite spring roll shop).

The atmosphere in the southern provinces was even more hostile. The south had always resented overrule from the Siamese kings in the north (first from Ayudhya, then from Bangkok). The people living there have a different character to the central Thais, being much more direct, much less polite, and much more overt about their dislike of foreigners. And they had no love for the Vietnamese who turned up on the beaches needing help.

As the Communist regime in Vietnam gradually exerted its control over the South through 1975, former Government officials and soldiers were rounded up and sent to re-education camps, with any who had taken part in particularly violent campaigns during the war being singled out for

severe treatment. (An example was the CIA-backed Phoenix programme which ran from 1967 to 1972 and was designed to identify and destroy the communist Viet Cong, officially known as the National Liberation Front of South Vietnam and backed by the North Vietnamese Army.)

The first to escape on boats were either people who had

yet to be identified as being part of the defeated regime and wanted to avoid re-education, or some who had escaped from detention, and their families. They secretly acquired old fishing boats at villages along the coast and in the Mekong delta, and as long as they could evade capture, or bribe the police or military if they could not, set off West towards Thailand.

Any that tried to get through Cambodian waters failed, most likely captured and disposed of by the Khmer Rouge. In three years only one small boat that arrived in Southeast Thailand reported coming that way, and when I was in Trat, gunfire could frequently be heard at night from the islands off the Cambodian coast, it was presumed targeting, mainly, smugglers.

Initial numbers were small. When I first arrived at Songkhla there were some 200 people squeezed into a tiny area barely the size of half a football pitch on a patch of land between the police station and the harbour. To call it a camp was an exaggeration. It was an eyesore, a collection of dirty huts that the Vietnamese had put together themselves from bamboo, planks, driftwood, plastic sheeting, tin cans, corrugated iron sheets, and whatever they could lay their hands on or, if they had money, what they could obtain from the local market. The camp was also visited by Catholic and Baptist missionaries, who were able to give limited material help and who, among other things, acted as a lifeline postal service.

My first visit to the camp was preceded by the customary official calls on the Governor and the Police Chief. Both made it very clear that they did not like the Vietnamese, did not want them in their province, and that the UN should remove them. The Police Chief, whose office directly overlooked the site, was particularly hostile towards me, but fortunately one his staff, a sergeant who had been given the task of actually overseeing the camp, was a lot more sympathetic once I had explained that I had come to interview the Vietnamese so they could be resettled overseas.

The immediate and unanswerable question was, how long would it take? Escorted by Police Sergeant Chalerm, I entered the camp and was quickly surrounded by anxious refugees holding their identity papers, as well as any evidence of relatives abroad. The camp had created a leadership hierarchy that had an elected committee whose members appeared to reflect their former social standing in Vietnam. They were usually very well organized, and many of them spoke passable English.

I explained that I would need to set up an interview programme starting with the committee members themselves and left them to arrange the rest. I estimated that if there were some 75 family groups in the camp, each interview would take 30-45 minutes for the basic information to be recorded, so that implied at least 5-7 full-time days of work in a space perhaps

8' x 12' that served as the camp "office". I obviously needed a translator, and immediately the committee identified a couple of people they thought suitable, we were introduced, and we set to work.

The internal organisation of the camps was arranged by the camp committee, elected or appointed by the refugees themselves. There was always a head of camp, whose responsibility it was to be the main contact with the Thai authorities and any visitors to the camp, so had a lot of authority within the camp. The committee kept very detailed records of new arrivals, partly to investigate whether there were any suspected or real communists among them, to find out the latest news from Vietnam, and to record details of their journey. They were quick to understand what information was needed for the interviews (with both the UN and the various immigration teams), and this saved a lot of time.

Any complaints about bad treatment or perceived injustices from the Thai guards, if they couldn't be sorted out between them, were passed up to the camp head, who would then report a sanitised or exaggerated version to me, often in written form. We were usually able to come up with practical solutions to the issues that emerged, which were most frequently related to the refugees' resettlement prospects, but also could be with the quality of the food they received (delivered by local Thai merchants contracted to the provincial government office, which received its funds from The Ministry of Interior in Bangkok, which was funded by the UNHCR), or with incidents of robbery in the camp, or with personal vendettas, or with trouble from the Thai guards. Over the years I worked with many heads of camps and developed good relationships with all of them, obviously some better than others, and corresponded with quite a few after they had left.

Vegetable distribution in the old Songkhla camp

The Field Officer role also covered peace-keeping, not in a typical UN geopolitical sense, but one of trying to defuse the simmering tensions and frustrations amongst the refugees, whether caused by imagined or real injustices on the part of the Thais (the Vietnamese were always quick to perceive injustices), or from treatment by the visiting immigration teams from the Embassies, or from the frequent internal denunciations and accusations that were a feature of life in the camp. However, the discipline within the camps was generally good, the Vietnamese themselves appearing to be able to maintain reasonable order, although this varied depending on the quality of the leadership team, the degree of influence it had, and the number of people in the camp with pronounced anti-social tendencies.

Overall, everyone seemed to be aware that bad or reckless behaviour might jeopardise the chances of quick resettlement (which in some cases it did) or induce harsher treatment from the Thais. I would often receive hand-written notes from refugees about some incident, frequently concerning a presumed theft of personal belongings, and the committee or camp chief would sometimes raise issues they thought better handled by the UN or that the UN should take up with the Thais. At the same time the missionaries were always ready to report on – and often exaggerate – incidents in the camp, and such cases always needed further investigation.

I took the view that I could not afford to get too embroiled in camp life, and as the committees made an effort to present an outward face that things were in order, I was no doubt kept ignorant of most of the goings-on, of which there must have been plenty given the crowded conditions in the camps.

When I was in Songkhla, I always stayed at the Samila Hotel, situated beside the beach about a mile from the centre of town. It was comfortable, but fairly basic, and had been built some time before. It had a pool that was rarely clean enough to use, but the sea was so close and was a very good place to swim in the season when the monsoon wasn't blowing directly in. The hotel restaurant was adequate, but never changed its limited menu, so usually in the evening we would either go into town where there were a few excellent seafood restaurants (one in particular), or more frequently, walk down the beach behind the hotel where there were several small restaurants pitched on the sand.

The biggest and best of these we called the Seven Sisters, run by a woman with seven daughters ranging from the eldest, who effectively ran the restaurant, to the youngest, who was still at school. I was such a regular customer, and was very often accompanied by visitors, that the mother suggested I should take her third (I think) daughter as my local wife.

I explained the impracticality of it, that I travelled a lot, and that I didn't know how long I would be staying in Thailand, etc. but she nonetheless thought it a great idea and said that her daughter thought so too. The daughter in question was a lovely girl, intensely shy, who was always deeply embarrassed to see me, and with whom I don't recall ever having a proper conversation. It was never an invitation that I considered at all seriously, but it provided an endless source of good-humoured teasing by the mother (of both her daughter and I).

Over the three years I was based in Songkhla, I had count-less wonderful seafood dinners there, sitting in deckchairs under the stars, drinking beer and talking into the night. It was a favourite place to take the many visitors who came down to visit the camp – immigration teams, journalists, NGO's, and consulate or embassy staff.

During my time in the South I always hired the same driver, Surat, whom I met outside the Samila hotel the first day I arrived in Songkhla. He was a local man, a Moslem, with an elderly Mercedes that he maintained in perfect condition. He became an invaluable source of information as well as something of a guardian angel. I often had to go to remote beach areas along the coast, often in Pattani and Narathiwat, the two most southerly coastal provinces in Thailand, both of which had predominantly Moslem populations.

These were areas of great poverty, small fishing villages with subsistence farming, largely ignored by the provincial Thai administration, which was usually Buddhist dominated. Every time we ventured into these remote areas, Surat would find out from the locals whether any Vietnamese had arrived, what had happened to them, and where they were.

Initially when it came to lunchtime, Surat would drop me off at a Thai or Chinese restaurant in the nearest town, and he went off elsewhere. I deduced very quickly that he would only eat at Muslim restaurants and told him that I would like to do

so as well. He thought I wouldn't or couldn't eat Moslem food, but once I had proven that both assumptions were misplaced, we thereafter ate together, which seemed to give him great satisfaction. It particularly pleased me, since the meals were always good, if usually very basic, depending on the town or village we happened to be in.

He was always responsible for taking the share of supplies to the heads of the villages closest to where the Vietnamese had landed. And he was always very concerned for my safety. One time we had gone up to Pakpanang, following a lead that refugees had arrived there. The province of Nakorn Sri Thammarat was (and perhaps still is) notorious for its dislike of outsiders, especially foreigners and people from Bangkok. I called in at the police station and was told that at the time there were no Vietnamese in the area, and when the police chief learnt that I was staying the night in the town, he advised me not to leave the hotel. Surat repeated this advice and made sure that we had an early supper and that I was back in the hotel before it got dark.

Another time we were coming back a bit later than intended from Panare, a village south of Pattani, when the car broke down on the highway just as it was getting dark. I had been warned by the governor of Songkhla to be off the roads by nightfall – the security at the time was not good, with communist and separatist insurgents active in the provinces of Pattani, Yala, and Narathiwat, this combined with widespread general banditry, so night-time attacks on vehicles were relatively common.

Surat couldn't get the car started again, and it was the only time that I saw him seriously worried. Luckily, a car heading north came by which he flagged down, and even more luckily, he knew the driver, another taxi owner from Songkhla, and agreed with him to take me back to the hotel, which he duly did. I was relieved the following morning to see a smiling Surat waiting for me outside the hotel as usual.

Soon after I arrived in the South, the office asked me to prepare a brief report on how the Vietnamese were organising their trips. I reported as follows:

Departures from Vietnam.

Means by which people leave Vietnam vary widely, as do their motivations for doing so. Attention here is focussed on some of the methods used by people in Saigon/Cholon to effect their escape.

*(1) **Sailing direct from the city**. Very rare and only in exceptional circumstances (such as a family of 4 who built their own boat)*

*(2) **Use of middleman**. Involved payment to a 3rd party, often unseen, who – as far as possible – guarantees an escape. (Much used by wealthier Chinese who arrange for their children to leave). A lumpsum payment will include organisation and transportation and no further payment is usually necessary, but the system is easily and often abused by contacts who disappear with the money.*

*(3) **Offshore transfer**. A contacts B in (say) Cholon. Both have relatives or friends overseas. A's friend will make a payment to B's relative in (say, the USA or Hong Kong) and B will then organise the escape. This method obviously limited to those with good enough overseas contacts.*

*(4) **Sequential payments**. Can be in varying number of stages – e.g. (i) for the initial contact, (ii) for movement to the coast, (iii) at embarkation, (iv) in international waters, (v) at country of temporary haven etc. This system open to every kind of abuse and often never-ending: threats of throwing overboard if price not increased; forced indebtedness through promises to pay more once resettled in a*

third country; outright robbery of everything once on the boat, etc.

(5) Transfer at sea. Vietnamese fishing boats are used to transport refugees to a pre-arranged (or not, as the case may be) location where transfer to a Thai (or Malaysian, or Indonesian or Philippine) fishing boat which will then either take them to a deserted spot on the coast and leave them (and usually robbing them of any remaining valuables), or drop them off somewhere along the coast, some of whom may find their way into a camp. But others do not. The Vietnamese boat would then go back to fishing and return to Vietnam for the next trip. Often this kind of transfer is not foreseen in the original plans, and there is no guarantee of survival after the transfer. Contacts between Thai and Vietnamese fishermen are more frequent than commonly supposed and a lot of smuggling goes on between the fishing fleets. (Thais take goods scarce in Vietnam to exchange for permission to fish the richer grounds off the Vietnamese coast).

(6) Individual efforts. Through bribery (for purchase of false travel documents, movement to the coast, plus further payment for a boat, or boat plus a fisherman, who may or may not take his family along).

There are obviously variations to each of the above-mentioned methods. More than a few people arrive saying that they had been picked up by a Thai fishing boat because their own boat was sinking. Many more arrive without papers or documentation, claiming that Thai pirates/ fishermen/police had taken them. These papers presumably have some kind of value, so we need to beware of non-Vietnamese Chinese arriving in the areas with seemingly valid documentation.

It was impossible to categorise the Vietnamese beyond basic family or individual identities – they quickly became just statistics, the arrival of their boats and the numbers on board noted and shared. The following telegram from the US Consulate in Songkhla, which would have obtained its information either from me or directly from the camp, is an example of the terse reporting that was the norm:[7]

Telegram from the Embassy in Thailand to the Department of State
3874. Following sent fm Songkhla
dtd 17 Feb 77 repeated for your info.

Subject: More Refugees Arrive in Songkhla.
1. After a lull in January, refugee boat arrivals have picked up this month. Two most recent arrivals are boat of ten from Rach Gia which arrived Feb 10, and boat of nineteen from Phu Quoc which arrived Feb 14. Many of the refugees on the boat from Phu Quoc have relatives in the U.S.

2. Recent arrivals say that although fuel shortages and tighter shore patrols have cut down on the numbers of refugees able to escape, hundreds more are planning to try to make the attempt. They predicted an increase in attempted escapes beginning around Tet and continuing for about three months when the sea is at its calmest.

3. There are rumors circulating in the Songkhla camp that insurgents may attempt to cause some disturbance there during Tet. This is probably generated by refugees themselves and seem unlikely. Camp is located directly across from the district police station.

---

7. https://history.state.gov/historicaldocuments/frus1977-80v22/d153

> *4. Camp population is now at about 650. This is down from a high of almost 1000 due primarily to fact that Australians, French, and West Germans have taken sizeable numbers from Songkhla in the past month".*

While the raw boat statistics were collated and circulated in a cold factual way, to me, each boatload meant interviews with every individual and family who arrived. While all were relieved and grateful to have made it into a UN-sponsored camp and be talking to a UN representative who represented their first step towards a new life, many had been severely traumatised by their passage from Vietnam. In present-day terms, most would likely have been suffering from Post-Traumatic Stress Disorder, which no-one at the time was qualified to recognise or diagnose, let alone treat.

One of the results of this was that false claims of relationships, imaginative biographical information and fabricated backgrounds were very common. It was widely known that US Immigration gave preference to ex-South Vietnamese military or government staff, to those who had worked with the Americans in Vietnam, or who had close relatives already in the US. The preliminary investigative work would be carried out by the camp committee which would sift through the personal stories and the information provided, before the arrivals were presented to the UN, and usually we did not attempt to probe too deeply.

The UNHCR interview process was therefore an essential and important first step in establishing not only who they were, but also whether or how easily they might qualify for resettlement in a third country. The interview forms that I re-designed and had to complete in camp were taken to Bangkok, copied, and sent to the various embassies, where the information I had recorded was subsequently verified as far

as possible by the respective immigration teams. I could never claim (and never did) that my notes were 100% accurate, but I took the view that as long as a story was consistent with what I'd learned or heard before, and that the family looked like a coherent unit, then it was a good place to start.

Where necessary, I noted that the information was un-verifiable, that I thought the person was lying, or that there was some other warning sign. In the end it didn't matter that much in terms of any refugee's future, since there was never a question that any of the Vietnamese would be allowed to stay in Thailand, and all were ultimately destined, sooner or later, for resettlement overseas. Despite this, they were quite adept in modifying their stories to appear of higher priority. Due to the Thai authorities' incessant, if varying, degree of hostility, there was always considerable pressure to get any new arrivals registered in the UN system as fast as possible so, inevitably, inaccuracies must have got into the documentation.

5

Change of Guard

When I first arrived in Thailand the head of the UNCHR in Bangkok, the Regional Representative, was a very experienced and principled Italian Swiss, Cesare Berta. He had served for many years in the organisation, was a kind man with a rich repertoire of anecdotes, and who was always ready to give sound advice. He allowed his three roaming field officers a lot of freedom, no doubt largely because he had little effective means of controlling us since communications were so poor. Also, he had not worked in Asia before, and was unusually prepared to listen to what we thought was going on.

His deputy was Nicholas Morris, a former New Zealand navy officer who was very organised, wrote extremely articulate reports to headquarters in impeccable English (and whose very clear and distinctive handwriting was instantly recognisable). He had spent a lot of time in the Middle East, had been posted in the New York office before arriving in Thailand, his first posting in Asia, where his normal straightforward approach wasn't always suited to the shifting tides of Thailand. He became a regular squash partner whenever I was passing through Bangkok.

The third of the leadership team was Werner Blatter, the cynical Swiss who had first introduced me to the Northeast. By autumn 1977, all three had departed to other posts, their

Cesare Berta

Nicholas Morris

Martin Barber (in Klong Yai Camp)

Pierre Jambor

places taken by Leslie Goodyear, a laidback Englishman who was appointed as the new representative (and again, someone who had never worked in Asia), and two deputies who were a bit younger than the people they replaced, and therefore closer to my own age.

Martin Barber, a serious and scholarly St. Andrews University graduate who had worked in Laos before with UNHCR and spoke the language, and Pierre Jambor, a Tunisian-born Italian with a Hungarian father and Italian mother, who arrived from a posting with UNHCR in Hanoi, and who was warm-hearted, curious and outgoing.

The immediate result of the clear-out at the top was that the field officers became, *de facto*, the most locally experienced voices and most reliable sources of field information in the office. Since we all operated at a distance, we tended to become even more autonomous. Goodyear was a decent man, but perhaps a typical career bureaucrat; cautious, indecisive, and never looking for a hill to fight on. Fortunately, the relationships with the two new deputies became very close, and we developed a strong friendship and trust.

Letter home 24 November 1977

Some three weeks ago, the Thais decided that they would adopt a new "get tough" policy towards the boat refugees. In some respects it was predictable, for they had refused to register any the new arrivals in either of the two camps [in Songkhla and Chantaburi] since the middle of September...
I had been a few days in Bangkok on routine business, and on return to the Songkhla camp was greeted with the spectacle of army trucks; police and Government officials loading all recently-arrived Vietnamese onto the vehicles which took them to an army camp 4 kilometres out of town. They were worried, especially when they saw their new

*lodgings – 2 open-sided 20x5 metre tents for 517 people …
in monsoon weather.*

*The Thais later that evening showed a taste of things
to follow when they tried to force 18 people to leave on a
boat which had arrived in the port and was about to be
expelled. They decided to stand firm, so all remained until
the next day, by which time everybody had been banned
from the new location. While they were only supposed to be
there until their boats were made seaworthy, their stay was
prolonged by further damage which made them unfit to sail
(the boats had been anchored off the old camp, which still
contained the older arrivals).*

*I was also banned from the site, even after direct appeal
to the local authorities who did, however, relent when an
American immigration team arrived the following day, and
were permitted entry only when they guaranteed to take as
many as possible, as quickly as possible… and there began
a long, long, week. The procedure that had been set up
was that UNHCR had to pre-screen all arrivals, so I had to
interview upwards of 300 people in 2 or 3 days in order to
present them to US immigration, who were on a very tight
schedule. The Vietnamese were terrified, guarded as they
were by soldiers with loaded M-16's and grenade launchers,
and exposed to the rains in their inadequate shelter.*

*So we worked well into the night for 4 or 5 days, under
considerable emotional pressure. The Americans then left,
and the pressure to expel those not accepted then mounted
again. This led to my running around giving spurious promises to the Thais, comforting anxious Vietnamese, trying to
prevent the pilfering that had started in the camp (and that
later developed into larger-scale robbery by the guards),
and spending long hours trying to persuade the authorities
to distribute food to the refugees. Then, a return to Bangkok*

to say farewell to the head of the office and greet the new one (a slightly weak Englishman with a Greek wife) who appeared to be surprisingly relaxed about the situation. An immediate return to Songkla accompanied by my new chief plus one of the directors from Geneva, then a visit to the other camp [in Chantaburi] where the same nonsense [of forced expulsion] started, was deferred, then started again.

The end result being enormous satisfaction, but great fatigue after 2 days off in 5 weeks ... I don't remember ever being pushed so far, so the experience has undoubtedly been valuable, however it is at times no great advantage to be saddled with a Judaeo-Christian conscience in "humanitarian affairs" in Asia. The sense of morality is very different from ours and it is not always easy to bridge the gap successfully. And the behaviour of the Vietnamese left much to be desired – only 2 days after they had been moved, they had to change their leadership due to factional in-fighting. Those who had helped with interpreting and arranging interviews were accused of favouritism and had to stand down. The entire episode has revealed much about character and characteristics. If you save someone who had fallen off a bridge, within 5 minutes he would be complaining that you hadn't managed to retrieve his parcels.

The Southern Thai is a very different creature from his Bangkok, Central or Northern colleagues, and it has been a good lesson in restraint from me to have to deal with some of the excesses – jumping up and crying would have brought even more irritations down on the heads of the Viets, and trying to explain my notions of responsibility and decency to people who historically detest the Vietnamese and who often take an undisguised delight in being able to treat them badly is not always easy to achieve. Having to smile

at people I dislike is a new experience and one which at
first was not very quick in coming, but now I'm learning and
am sure it will stand me in good stead.

Which of course, it did. And it also helped me to begin to learn
how to decipher the Thai smile that beguiles all the tourists
who go there. The adage that nothing is as it seems is especially
true of the Asian smile, and it took some time to be able to
discern sincerity when it appeared. It also provided a lengthy
field course in studying people's faces, wherever their origins.
And there was a constant flow of new faces to explore.

I recall one Field Officers meeting (in early 1978) that
Pierre had called in Bangkok, which all the key people in the
office attended, including the young Danish protection officer.
Subsequently we all went out for dinner together and once
Goodyear had retired for the evening, it struck me that everybody in the team was younger than 35. We were all highly
motivated, we were all working long hours in extremely
challenging circumstances, and we all believed that we were
striving for a worthwhile cause. It was an exhilarating and inspiring realisation, and in retrospect a pinnacle of satisfaction
I suppose rare in any career. It remained a high point of my
working life.

6

Off-duty exploits

Since I had to interview all the Boat People, it meant travelling between the camp in the south (Songkhla) and those in the southeast (at Laemsing, in Chantaburi province, and at Trat). I would complete the interviews, head back to Bangkok to deliver the forms to the office (from whence they would be sent to the various embassies), and then head out again down to the coast. In Songkhla I always stayed in the same hotel by the beach, the Samila, and in Chantaburi I stayed in the basic Travel Lodge hotel.

The other Field Officers had the convenience of a car and driver, and while I would occasionally have the use of an office car, my travel to Chantaburi was usually on the bus. An air conditioned "express" service ran every day, with a hostess who served sweet drinks and cake, but if it was full or had broken down, there was always the local orange bus. Natural ventilation through open windows, hard seats, it stopped more frequently, sometimes at the side of the road to pick up or drop off someone where a track emerged from the surrounding countryside. The drivers usually sported the glazed look of amphetamine use, and the buses were renowned for the speed they travelled at. Not surprisingly, accidents were not infrequent, especially at night. To get to the camp, I would hire a local taxi for the day.

Travel to Songkhla (via Haad Yai) airport was with Thai Airways, first encountered in my initial trip to the northeast. I became a regular on the southern route, and the twin propeller Avro 748's were gradually replaced by Boeing 737's on the longer domestic routes, which slashed the journey time. It was usually an uneventful trip, but monsoon season always increased the stress levels, since Thai Airways pilots had something of a reputation of "having a go" in bad weather conditions, especially those who had trained with the Royal Thai Air Force. Initially Haad Yai airport did not have the right radar for "blind" landings, and one particularly frightening trip stands out.

An evening flight from Bangkok in monsoon season with only a handful of passengers on board, we flew into a violent thunderstorm about half an hour out from Haad Yai. It was dark, the plane was flying through thick cloud, tossed around in all directions, the strapped-in stewardesses screaming every time there was another lurch. The pilot made an attempt to get down but had to abort and circle round again. A second attempt; same result. Prayers were said. Finally, a break in the cloud revealed the lights of the airport below and the pilot dived through the gap, hit the runway hard, and slithered to a halt beside the terminal in torrential rain. Relieved applause and smiles broke out, and I disembarked on shaking legs. (In April 1980, a Thai Airways 748 ran into a thunderstorm on approach to Khon Kaen, and crashed, killing most of the people on board.)

While we worked long and often intense hours in the field, the trips to Bangkok provided occasional opportunities for leisure activities, and it became a regular habit to visit one of the upmarket massage parlours where we could clean up and unwind. Dinner was a moveable feast, and while we had a few favourite restaurants, the quality and variety of food around town was invariably outstanding, including what could be discovered at street stalls. These were always basic but generally clean, although inevitably the occasional food poisoning and subsequent painful purge did occur. After dinner we would often drop in at a Patpong bar or two, where at a few of the better establishments we became recognised faces. It was all fun, and we played hard.

For the curious, Bangkok held endless interest, and having been told that the port area of Klong Toey was somewhat different, I decided one evening to go and explore. I took a taxi down to the darkened streets and found a dingy bar, where the staff were clearly astonished to see a young foreigner walk in, especially one who spoke some Thai. I stayed for a beer chatting to the girls, and at one stage the door opened and a dwarf, accompanied by a very young, very pregnant, girl came in and approached the tables. It wasn't clear which of them was soliciting sympathy for the other, and swiftly, one of the bar staff came round and escorted them to the door again. It was a surreal intrusion, and all that was said was that they came by 'often', the implication being that the girl had worked at the bar before. But I did not linger, making a discreet exit when I became aware of the increasingly hostile looks I was attracting from some of the tough-looking customers.

Another evening after dinner with a friend from the American Embassy, he suggested that we should take a look at where manual workers went for entertainment. He said he had been taken there by a Thai colleague, and seemed to know where to go, which was down a dark alley close to Sanam Luang in the centre of the old city. It was like a descent into Dante's Inferno. We attracted a lot of attention, overhearing a couple of locals opining that we must have been drunk. Our destination was what was euphemistically called a massage parlour, where several hundred girls were sitting in a brightly lit room, ogled at by hundreds of would-be customers. There was steady stream of girls going in and out, to meet or return from an encounter with whichever man had called out their number. It was a sobering experience, and despite the enthusiastic offers of a manager, we extricated ourselves from the crowd and returned to a quieter part of town.

For a brief period, David and I decided to rent a house in Chantaburi for a few months to get away from the hotel atmosphere where we were always under scrutiny, but it didn't work out since neither of us were there either often enough or for very long. Instead, we decided to rent an apartment in Bangkok so we could have somewhere to stay when passing through town, and that turned out to be a good decision. We rarely overlapped, and it at least gave us somewhere to call home base.

Letter home 16 January 1978
My (Bangkok) domestic base has moved (again). The previous house was not altogether suitable and was prone

to having no water (5 days out of 6) which was irritating, especially when the lane outside was flooded. Added to that major inconvenience, the maid (whom we had taken on with the house as part of a favour to an erstwhile colleague) was a lazy old nonsense who spent most of her time watching television when she thought we weren't there. So we were extremely lucky and found a new place, very centrally located, swimming pool, reasonably congenial neighbours apart from an Israeli diplomat with 4 very noisy small children, and a charming aristocratic owner with a beautiful and even more charming foreign-educated daughter.[8]

---

8. Obviously unaware to me at the time, the daughter, a very attractive girl who had been educated in France, and whose parents were trying to arrange a suitable society marriage for her, was to play a pivotal role in my life nearly ten years later in 1987, when I bumped into her at a reception at the Hilton Hotel in Bangkok. She happened to be the only person I knew there, and she introduced me to her friend whom she knew from her days in Paris. This friend had earned a PhD in law from the Sorbonne University, was French-speaking, very attractive, extremely intelligent, worked for the government, and, to cut a lengthy story very short, some time later became my wife and the mother of my children.

Life did not entirely revolve around refugees and the UNHCR, and there were moments of relaxation and time for an occasional holiday. David Jamieson and I flew to Hong Kong for a weekend in 1976 on a 747 operated by a private airline called Air Siam. The airline had not confirmed the return trip but had assured us that it would not be a problem. When we got to the airport in Hong Kong to return to Bangkok, there seemed to be an awful lot of people in the same situation. We tried to play the UN card with the Thai station manager, saying that it was vitally important that we got back, but he was far more interested in attending to the stream of Thais with multiple suitcases filled with their weekend's shopping in Hong Kong, whom he would invite into a back office. Shortly afterwards they would return, all smiles, to check in. We were naïve enough to think that we might be given the last seats on the plane, but when the flight was closed in our faces, we ended up having to get an expensive Swissair flight instead, giving us another costly lesson in survival in Asia. Despite that, going from the austerity of upcountry Thailand to the luxury and linen sheets of the Mandarin Hotel was a striking contrast.

In December that year I spent 10 days in Sri Lanka with the family of an old friend from University, David Gordon, and in mid-1977, Hank Hendrickson and I went to Penang for 10 days of golf, tennis, sailing and swimming. We had intended to head up to the Cameron Highlands as well, but the ambience, activities, and company we found at the Rasa Sayang hotel on Batu Ferringi (nowadays part of the Shangri-La chain) proved to be too attractive to explore any further, and we never made it. Later that year, at Christmas, Pierre Jambor, David Jamieson and I decided to get out of Bangkok at short notice, and so bought tickets for a 3-day trip to Nepal. The same letter home described the visit:

Letter home 16 January 1978

My trip to Nepal ... was an unqualified success from the moment we landed until we disembarked in Bangkok some three and a half days later. I deliberately omit the flight there – I think it was the only time I have ever landed with the plane accelerating fast at the precise moment of touchdown .. for our Royal Nepal Airlines pilot was going to put us down in a field before the runway began. But we bounced, bumped, shuddered up the runway and came to a handbrake stop in front of the terminal building, and on descending from the plane the sensations began. A cool, clear night with near full moon, a world away from the stale fetid air of Bangkok.

I had seen pictures in Kathmandu in a book, and thought it interesting and quaint, and had heard many first-hand accounts of the country, but nothing could have prepared me for that first night's walk out of the hotel, into the old town and into 500 or 1000 years of history. The impact of that first venture into the unknown was to be repeated many times in next few days; so many vivid, unique memories. An extraordinary concentration of emotions, people, smells, and visions which all combined to dazzle and engrave themselves into a truly marvellous experience.

So many stand out: the magic of standing on a ridge at 7000 feet and watching the sun come up and the mist up to our waists streaming out of the valley to the East; sitting atop a hill in a temple overlooking the Kathmandu valley and watching the sun set, igniting the peaks in the distance; stumbling through deserted areas of the old city in near blackness, and looking inside houses unchanged in centuries.

Our flight back was a riot, and due to overcrowding we found ourselves sitting aft of the cabin where the crew usually sit. We were flying on Thai International, the cabin staff poured champagne down our throats, and we made a brief stop-over at Calcutta where the Norwegian captain (seconded to Thai from SAS) publicly and volubly cursed the Indians for always being late, as they were on that occasion too. But no matter, it put the cap on an excellent Christmas weekend.

There were also off-duty visits to the north, to visit Mouchet in Nan, and to Chiang Saen, Chiang Rai, and Mae Hong Son close to the Burmese border, from where we drove over the thickly forested hills to Pai village on an unpaved road that was still being cut. Breaking through the early morning clouds, we could see range after range of untouched jungled mountains stretching north as far as the eye could see. At the time Pai had almost no out-of-province visitors, and the only thing we could find to eat there was a bowl of delicious fresh fragrant rice. Nowadays, the district is firmly on the tourist trail, no doubt its former tranquillity lost forever.

Before David left Thailand for his new posting, he and I decided to take a trip to Taiwan and Korea. Taiwan was then under martial law, and although the former military dictator Chiang Kai-Shek had died in 1975, nightspots in the capital city, Taipei, were still subject to a curfew. Taipei was a fascinating mix of the old and new, with great food, and we spent a day visiting the extraordinary National Palace Museum which had been created in front of the mountain into which caves had been dug out to house the priceless treasures removed by the Kuomintang from the mainland in 1949 when they were defeated in the civil war with the Communists. We then took a bus down to the scenic Sun Moon Lake, where we took advantage of the hotel's offer of a massage, which was delivered – expertly – by an elderly blind masseuse.

We continued the trip on a hair-raising 2-day bus journey across the vertiginous Central Cross-Island Highway which was hacked out of the mountain cliffs (with considerable loss of life) by the Kuomintang troops evacuated from the mainland. The bus driver breezily told us that trucks were lost over the edge very year, and even stopped at one point to let us peer down into the deeps below where, sure enough, the wreckage of vehicles and their contents could be seen. (It has apparently since been closed to private vehicle traffic after a series of landslides caused by earthquakes and typhoons).

Only 90 miles wide, two thirds of the island is mountainous, with the tallest peak nearly 13,000 feet above sea level. We had an overnight stop at Dayuling, at an altitude of 8,400, where at the night market we bumped into a small group of attractive girls who, through one of the vendors who spoke a little English, suggested that we should visit them at their hotel. After a few discreet enquiries, it turned out that they were accompanying a group of Japanese businessmen who were out at dinner and not expected back until late. It was a tempting offer of local hospitality, but we quickly decided that avoidance of any possible incident with representatives of the

Taroko Marble Gorge

former colonial power would be the most sensible course of action, and so declined their kind offer. The next morning, we headed down the precipitous road through the spectacular marble Taroko Gorge to the Pacific coast, from where we caught a flight back to Taipei.

Having survived the perilous transit of Taiwan, we flew on to South Korea. Seoul at the time was also still under martial law and a strict curfew was in operation from midnight to 4am (it was only lifted in 1982). This resulted in one night spent in a bar that we did not get out of in time, which the staff took in a good-humoured way. As the Korea Times reported *"Even in Seoul, various bars and teahouses would close their doors at midnight with the patrons still inside, who would then while away the hours with food, drink, and conversation."*

7

Life gets more complicated

Letter home 17 April 1978

Some 300 new people have come in by boat to Trat province and await their interview with me, but that is a daily task and one I am glad to abandon each evening… The police chief of the neighbouring province here was two days ago killed in an ambush along with six other government workers. Not very comforting, especially when the inmates of the refugee camp in the province have now dug bunkers under their shelters. A town a few kilometres away is now being shelled and rocketed on a fairly regular, if light, basis. The camp itself is about 1 kilometre from the border and black shirted Khmer Rouge can be seen infrequently on the hill which dominates the site."

The period of relative calm between the fading of the Northeast and the re-emergence of the Southwest monsoons has meant a huge increase in the numbers of people arriving from Vietnam by boat. 250 in 6 days in Songkhla, 560 in one week in Malaysia. Today I ran into another 'interesting case'. A group of 4 men came to the interview claiming they were brothers. After 20 minutes they confessed that they were not even related, so they re-appeared as 2 cases, 3 brothers and a friend. This latter claimed he had arrived in Vietnam from Cambodia in mid-1975 and had then gone to high school (aged 21).

But a member of the committee claimed to have recognised him as having been in a regiment of the ARVN (S.

Vietnamese army) which had a high proportion of Vietcong infiltrators, and later that he saw him as police chief in a northern province of Vietnam after the fall of Saigon. So, while he claims he was at college, he was supposedly transferred to one of the southernmost provinces as head of the new regime's secret police … and in that role had subsequently been recognised by several others in the camp.

So why the subterfuge? Should one believe the voices in the camp, that he is/was a communist and has come amongst them to do ill deeds? Various factors weigh against him. By amazing coincidence, he managed to be quoted in Newsweek (under an alias) thereby becoming one of the very few refugees ever to have his name in the press. (Conspiracy theory: it was a pre-arranged signal). The family that brought him arrived intact with 10 children, some very small, and claimed that they had let him travel free.

But, (1) hardly any families arrive intact, especially with a large number of children and (2) even fewer people get out without paying something – in this case a guarantee that the family would be permitted to leave? There is a great temptation to construct an elaborate conspiracy theory out of it all, but I have to maintain an equilibrium (which, alas, is not all that apparent in an increasing number of the UN's dealings) and remain as unbiassed as possible.

We are also in the midst of an attempt to crack down on a racket which has been operated by the (Thai) camp chiefs who have been relieving the refugees of their boats and selling them for personal profit, while in Songkhla the refugees run a protection racket amongst themselves, denouncing their compatriots as Reds or drug smugglers etc. And so it goes on.

The conspiracy story is still unresolved. He gave 3 different names and 5 different stories, none of which

*coincided with the available facts: that he was a member
of the secret police in Rach Gia, one of the provinces that
see the most departures. But that was far from being the
only interesting tale, nor the only case of false identity and
obscure background."*

The increase in the numbers of arrivals in Thailand and
Malaysia led to a hardening of policy, and the Thai Government made it very clear that they would do all they could to
deter the boats. On one occasion in April 1978, a boat had
arrived south of Songkhla, having already been attacked
by fishermen, had been pushed back to sea, had then been
attacked again, and finally managed to run aground somewhere further south. The first I heard of it was a report that
a new group had been brought to the camp. It was a Sunday
morning, so the government offices were closed. I got to the
camp and discovered the group sitting in the open, outside
the camp.

I asked the head of the camp guards why they weren't
inside the camp, and he said he had been told to hold them
outside until the arrival of an important visitor from Bangkok,

who wanted to see them. Since the sun was up and getting hotter, and the refugees were in bad shape, I persuaded the guards to let people from the camp bring a tarpaulin for shelter, and water.

We waited, and meanwhile some of girls who had been raped at sea, fainted. With Dr. Pascal Gullety-Bosviel, a Medecins Sans Frontiers doctor who had come with me from the hotel, and a couple of the Vietnamese medics from the camp, we picked up the girls and carried them into the shelter of the guard house next to the camp. The one I was carrying weighed almost nothing and was still bleeding, and the doctor was able to give them essential medical care.

The hours passed. The heat intensified. The mood inside the camp was becoming increasingly hostile, the guards still didn't know when the visit would take place. The district officer appeared, and apologetically repeated that he could not authorise the transfer into the camp. Finally, around 4pm or perhaps a bit later, when the temperature was a bit cooler, a convoy of vehicles arrived and halted in a cloud of dust. From one of them emerged the portly figure of Thanat Khoman, a former Foreign Minister, signatory of the original ASEAN Treaty, and one of the more prominent political figures in Thailand.

I was hot, tired, hungry, frustrated, and angry. I approached the group and stood in front of them. The Governor of the Province, Chareonjit Na Songkhla, whom I knew and got on with quite well, explained who I was. Whereupon Thanat Khoman, in full pomposity with an audience of subordinates to perform to, launched into a tirade against the Vietnamese, against the UN, and against foreigners interfering with Thailand, and declaimed that "these people" (he gestured contemptuously at the Vietnamese slumped on the ground under their tarpaulin) would be thrown out. It was a disgraceful performance, as was the treatment of the Vietnamese, but I was dimly conscious that I occupied the moral high ground, and I knew that, nominally being Buddhists, the Thais would know it too.

I managed to stay calm, and while I don't recall now exactly what I said, it was words to the effect that the Thailand Government had asked for the UN's help, that the Vietnamese would all be resettled, that this group had been attacked and needed urgent medical attention and assistance, that they should be allowed into the camp, and that it was unworthy of Thailand to subject them to such treatment.

At this the Governor signalled for me to stop. Khoman by this time was puce in the face, visibly furious, and continued with his threats towards the Vietnamese and included me for good measure. The district officer took me aside and advised me to stay calm. The official visit continued, mercifully brief, and the party took off again. Later that night we managed to get the group into the camp, and the next morning I went to see the Governor to apologise for any embarrassment that the confrontation might have caused and get his permission for the group to stay. He was stern, but in fact quite understanding; he had already asked Bangkok for permission, and just said that we should try to get them interviewed and resettled as soon as possible.

A few days later, Dr. Gullety-Bosviel signed a brief statement, in French, a sad epitaph to a violent and unnecessary incident:

I, the undersigned Dr. Gullety-Bosviel, MD, A doctor with Medecins Sans Frontiers, responsible for medical care in the refugee camp of Songkhla have today examined:

Tong Oc Xuan   *15 years old*

Tong Oc Le	13 years old
Vo Bich Loan	20 years old
Truong Thi An	15 years old

And have diagnosed for these four young women a tearing of the hymen corresponding to rape some days earlier.
   Declared at Songkhla 26/4/78

As I had promised, all the group were eventually resettled overseas.

While this was intense enough, for some reason an account of the episode never featured in a letter home, perhaps because I didn't have time to write again until after another, perhaps even more dramatic incident.

Letter home 8 June 1978

I have been in the thick of things even more than usual, for a colleague went off on leave for 5 weeks and I had to cover part of his area for him. It led to rather an exciting evening in a town called Aranyaprathet, some five kilometres from the border with Cambodia. I had to go there at the beginning of May with a team from Canadian immigration (plus a TV crew from CBC) and while we were in the refugee camp near the town, we heard some muffled thumps in the distance.

It transpired that that morning, unbeknownst to us, the Khmer Rouge had staged strikes along the length of the border in the area, attacking many villages. The same after-noon, they decided to rocket, hence the "muffled thumps". When we returned to the town, we found that one rocket had landed 30 metres away from where we had had lunch, and another had crashed into the roof of the other hotel in town – about 100 metres up the street from our own.

A Thai aircraft went up and strafed suspected Khmer

positions and the occasional artillery burst could be heard. It later calmed down, and as my Canadian (Immigration) friend Ian Hamilton had never seen the border, we went out as far as we could to a roadblock, foolishly got out to take a look, but leaving again instants later after an AK47 started firing as we got back into the car. The Canadian was on the floor in 2 demi-seconds, and I was just behind him; the driver thought it was a firecracker until a second burst arrived and the nearby Thai troopers dived for cover, whereupon we accelerated away as fast as possible, casting nervous glances back at the border.

Back into town, where all was calm until about 17.00 when, in the middle of a well-earned beer, another rocker landed opposite the hotel, about 300 metres away. Much excitement, and like idiot tourists, up to the roof we went to get a better look. It was a splendid evening, the calm inter-rupted only by the occasional crump of outgoing artillery, when without warning (no whistle), a rocket landed about 150 metres away, again opposite the hotel and close enough to smell… we were off the roof and back on the ground floor in about 15 seconds, and a few moments later another rocket fell behind the hotel, close enough to break a window.

The TV crew had had the foresight to obtain a large icebox from a hotel in Bangkok, and this was crammed with beer. As darkness wore on, knuckles tightened slightly around the bottles which seemed to have only a marginal effect on one's thirst. Hotel guests then started to leave (including one of the senior Thai Army general staff), but we decided to stay on because it would have meant a round-trip of over 340 kilometres to go the nearest town and come back the next day.

We found the only restaurant open in town and retired early, since the town had largely been evacuated. In fact, the evening burst turned out to be the last for the day, we all slept soundly, and there were no further incidents the following day. That day was seemingly the worst attack on the town that has yet been, but border attacks are frequent, and two buses on roads that led very close to Cambodia were recently mined and machine-gunned. One of the difficulties is that the border is very ill-defined, and each side uses different maps, so it can lead to fatal confusion.

About two weeks later, the UN had a helicopter flight with some people from the Ministry of Interior from Aranya-prathet all the way along the Khmer border down to Trat. I can't say that that was a relaxed trip either, for the refugee camps are all very near border areas which are troubled by not infrequent incursions."

What I failed to mention in the letter home was that as we had driven into Aranyaprathet that morning, we had passed a long column of vehicles leaving the town. We found out later that the residents had been advised to evacuate, and the Thai military we had seen at the hotel had been ordered to fall back to the large military base at Wattana Nakhon, about 40 kilometres from the border.

In the hotel I bumped into a very attractive young Thai woman who, it turned out, had come up from Bangkok to meet the army officer we had seen hastily leaving the hotel. I suggested that she might like to share the protection of the UN (of which I happened to be the sole representative in the area) to which, happily, she agreed. So my night under the threat of further bombardment became instead an intimate and treasured memory. The next morning dawned sunny, fresh, and peaceful, and we headed back to the camp to work as originally intended.

· 8 ·
Festivals

After David Jamieson's departure, pending the appointment of a new field officer to the Eastern border, I would sometimes cover his area since I often travelled to Chantaburi in the Southeast. I would on such occasions use his vehicle and former driver, Supot, who suggested that I might like to visit his hometown in Yasothorn province (in the Northeast), where the annual rocket festival was about to take place. I had heard about the festival before, and as it was not too far to drive, I decided to go.

Letter home 8 June 1978

About 2 weeks ago I went up to a place called Yasothorn which was celebrating its annual "Boon Bang Fai". Essentially a fertility rite, it is always held at the onset of the rainy season in order to ensure a good rainfall and therefore plentiful crops. The Saturday was taken up with a procession through the streets of the town, each district or bank or village having its own teams of dancers leading a truck upon which is mounted their rocket, elaborately decorated and surrounded by the most beautiful girls in the village. Sometimes the trucks would be loaded with typical scenes – the rice paddy, or weavers; people of all ages participating.

The following day is given over to the ultimate symbol of all – the launching of the rockets. These come in various sizes, the biggest ones being up to 40 feet long, a tail of bamboo emerging from a steel tube into which is packed all kinds of explosive. The launch is sometimes very dangerous, and they can blow apart at the launching-tree. Others go straight into the air for hundreds of feet, and usually the prize is awarded to the rocket that stays airborne the longest.

While the Saturday was very hot and sunny, the Sunday was gloomy and very wet, but this had no effect on the spirit of the ceremonies, even if the dampness of some of the rockets made them hiss and spew smoke in all direction rather than ignite and take off, and in no way subdued the locals who were rushing around in the half-flooded paddy fields trying to cover the nearest victim in mud. Preferably by means of rolling him in it. I was the only foreigner there and was probably quite lucky to escape with only wet feet.

They all speak a Lao dialect up there, and under the tutelage of my driver, whose parents' home was only a few kilometres away, I was able to be less of a stranger to

them. Such phrases as "hak sao Yaso dee lai" guaranteed immediate attention and fits of laughter from the younger women. (Roughly translated, it means "I like Yasothon girls very much"). Supot, (the driver, who I assumed had some experience in the matter) assured me that Yasothon girls were renowned for their willingness to "tiao" (enjoy themselves), but alas, we were unable to stay and put it to the test. Instead, he took me to visit his parents in the back of beyond, in a village until only about 5 years ago closed to the outside world – i.e. no roads; and even now the road is just a dirt-track punctuated with holes. His nephews and nieces were fascinated and terrified by such a large white person, and his mother was in the middle of making mango toffee, welcoming us with a hot slab … and a cold beer.

The Thais were not alone in celebrating festivals. In the camps, the refugees would make special efforts for, especially, their

New Year festivals, Songkran in the Lao camps, Tet in the Vietnamese. We would be invited to attend, and even in the cramped conditions of the Vietnamese camps, a modest feast would be prepared, usually of remarkably high quality. The occasions would sometimes also double up as farewell dinners for departing camp chiefs, and they were also a very good means for offering hospitality to the Thai officials, especially the police in charge of the camps.

9

The interpreters

I always used an interpreter from amongst the camp population because they invariably knew what was going on in the camp and what was being talked about. Each new arrival would be vetted by the camp committee, which noted their details, point of departure etc. and took a view of their bona fides, passed on to me informally as required. I usually selected one of the younger refugees who had already been, or was highly likely to be, approved quickly for resettlement, mainly because the younger ones were less likely to be involved in the (incessant) camp intrigues, they were slightly more naïve, and also because their English was often better than many of their older refugees.

The working conditions were difficult and often intense, but my interpreter assistants were always patient, well turned out, and what I would call remarkably professional in approach. As a result, I got to know them quite well and developed quite close relationships with them.

Friendships with the refugees required caution and discretion, since I had to maintain, and be seen to maintain, as neutral a position in the camp as possible, and any suggestion of favouritism could have rebounded badly. It wasn't that I didn't develop strong likings for some of the people in the camps – there were some very likeable and robust personalities amongst them, and everybody had an interesting story to tell. But I was very conscious that everything I did was closely

With another excellent interpreter, Cho Van Tran (in blue shirt)

observed and that there were constant attempts to manipulate me emotionally.

I don't remember now the exact number of interpreters I worked with over three years in the two camps, there were many, but three individuals, from the Songkhla camp, stand out in the memory in particular, mainly because with each of them, I kept up correspondence for a few years after they had left the camp.

The first was Trang Van Duong, a highly intelligent young woman who spoke excellent French and good English, who left the camp at the end of 1977. Next was Hung T. Mai, a very bright engineer, who left for the USA in June 1979; and the third was Hoang Thi Le Thuy, an even younger woman who emigrated with her brother to the USA in late 1979.

The following selected extracts from the letters they sent give a varied picture of their early steps in their new lives.

First, Trang Van Duong, who wrote a series of amusing and slightly teasing letters (my translation from her original, extremely good, French):

Bangkok, 14 Jan 1978 – *"As you know, I left Songkhla on December 28th ... I thought of writing to you to say goodbye but didn't have time and thinking that once in Bangkok it wouldn't be difficult to see you... I don't think I will leave without seeing you, but if that happens, I will surely write to you from the US even if you don't reply... I'm infinitely grateful for everything you have done for me and above all for your advice..."*

Rockville MD, 24 Jan 1978 – *"It's already a week since I arrived here ... it snowed last night and is still snowing – it's marvellous! ... I'm waiting to enter university in August. In the meantime, I eat, I sleep, and I go out every day with my sponsor who adores me and gives me everything that I want. Poor fellow, he will ruin himself in the end. But seriously, I must still take English and secretarial lessons. Freedom is beautiful, but expensive!"*

Rockville MD, 14 April 1978 – *"...You were nearly right to say that I was going to become "an all-American babe". In truth, I like hamburgers, but don't eat them every day because I'm on a diet (which is also very American). I watch TV 24/24 but still don't understand "base-ball". I've already bought myself a car, an American brand of course, only I don't yet have a license because I still can't reverse, and I have problems with "parallel parking". I've also had problems with my sponsor; he certainly spoils me, but he also knows how to be very demanding, and asks too much of me and I'm fed up with his whims."*

Washington DC, 11 June 1978 – *"I've finally finished my computer course after 6 months of relentless work. I received my diploma last month – with honours of course! But the most important thing is that three weeks ago I already found a job and am now an employee of a company that has a 6-month contract with the Department of Labour in Washington. My work is very interesting and the salary not too bad. I'm a junior programmer, and if I do well enough, in a year my future should be very good…Before ending, a small suggestion that if you want to have a change of work and make a fortune in future, "data processing might be interesting to you".*

Rockville MD, 30 August 1978 – "I've had a lot of work these past few months, day and night, so much so that I had to go and see a doctor who prescribed a few days of rest, the charming man! Do you know that my sponsor has promised to buy me an air ticket to Paris, and even a tour of Europe if I make an effort to spoil and pamper him? I assure you, my friend, I'm not going to stay here much longer… Here in Rockville my brother and some friends have just organised a modest organisation to find voluntary sponsors for refugees in Thailand and Malaysia. At the moment we are awaiting a fishing family of 13 people from Malaysia.

Rockville MD, 26 April 1979 – "… My work occupies more and more of my time, and I think I must have aged 10 years in the last 4 months. Did I tell you that I had received a promotion in January? My boss is satisfied enough with me, and to prove it piles more work on me up to my neck. But since the salary is not too bad, and since no Texan millionaire has come to ask me to marry him, I must do my best."

[I subsequently met up with Duong on my trip across the USA in 1979 when I went to stay in Washington DC. I don't remember much detail about the visit but do recall that we spent a very agreeable afternoon together driving around the nearby countryside which she was keen to show me. The correspondence took up again after I had started work in Geneva.]

Rockville MD, 15 May 1980 – "…So you're looking to leave the UN? Will you go into business or go back to school? It's strange, since I know tons of people whose dream is to work for the UN, and on the contrary, you want to get out. I'm in a similar situation, the company I work for is big enough, the benefits are good, and yet I'm looking to change, since I'm beginning to get bored. "I'm sick of programming. I think I want to get into sales. I also want to take a vacation". I don't think that I can give myself the luxury of a trip to Europe this year, because I've just sent some money to my mother in Vietnam to help her get out of the country, hopefully".

Amsterdam, 1 September 1980 – "As you can see, I'm writing from Holland, where my company has sent me for at least 5 months. I hadn't expected to be sent to Europe, and I jumped at the opportunity… I'm so excited at the idea of being able to travel to France, Belgium, England and Switzerland as easily as going from New York to Montreal.

Amsterdam, 18 September 1980 – "On the 26th of this month I will be in Paris, and I would cordially like to invite you to come to my and my sister's birthday with my family."

Amsterdam, 13 November 1980 – "The next time I will be in Paris will be 15 December, and I hope that this time we will be able to meet… I've sometimes thought about going back to university but lack the courage. In any case, I certainly don't lack work, especially in October, when we were working 12 hours a day plus at weekends. Happily, from now until the end of the year the pressure is easing off as the contract comes to an end. It's why I'm being sent back to the US at the end of December for a few months. Another

*contract is due to be signed around March 1981, and at that
point I'll return to Holland for 3 years. I hope!"*

The second was Hung The Mai (seen below on the left with
the camp chief), a qualified engineer around my own age and
married with a wife and young daughter in the camp, and
who was fairly swiftly accepted by the US. His English was
very good, and he went first to Hawaii, where I caught up with
him in September 1979 when I stopped off en route to the US
on my way home after leaving Thailand. He later moved to
Tampa in Florida. We exchanged letters for a number of years,
and I was able to follow both his struggles and his progress.

*Lumpini Transit Centre, June 16 1979 – "My family has left
Songkhla on June 11, we had a terrible trip, we encountered
more than 10 times troubles by buses. It took us over 28*

hours to get to Bangkok. ... In the near future I will go to Hawaii therefore I am far from you forever. I hope that one day we are together on another position. Thank you very much for your help during the period I stayed in Songkhla, I will remember your help everlasting"

Honolulu June 24th '79 – "In the new community which is very large and manifold like America I'm really worry about my life in present time and in future...It's very clear for me if I would like to have a stable life I have to continue studying. I intend to get professional engineer and after that I will study Master Engineering, if possible."

Hawaii July 5th 1979 – "I have been here 16 days. Up til now I am unemployment. I try to look for a job and an apartment for rent. The Americans here have prejudice and despised the Vietnamese refugees. I can't rent an apartment if I have no job. I still intend to continue my education... In period of hopeless, I always remember you and write to you. Do you have any advice for me?"

Hawaii July 17th 1979 – "One month and a week I have left Songkhla refugee camp ... Tomorrow I will go to get an apartment with 3 bedrooms from Housing Authority and will move to new shelter very soon. I also applied about five companies and associates for my job and I hope I will get a job although it won't suitable with my ability.

Honolulu Aug 14th 1979 – "I have moved to the new apartment since Aug 1st ... I have had a job in SAM O. HIROTA. This company is a consultant engineer. My position is Engineer Aide. Salary $700/month that's O for a refugee. My wife and my brother have attended English class".

Honolulu November 28th 1979 – "On this occasion I need your help too. I have received some information about my relatives who escaped from Vietnam but up til now I don't know where they are. My wife said "only Mr. Lean can help us". So I give you some information about my relatives…" [I was able to respond on 17th December with details of his relatives]

Honolulu December 30 1979 – "My family still live in a normal condition, I still work in the old employer and I plan to take the Engineer-in-Training exam next April 1980. My wife will get a scholarship and will go to college so that she can learn English about 6 months or one year after that she will study a vocational course……My life now is no meaning I think, I try to work for my children. You asked about my hopes and fears in the new decade. Of course I hope a lot of things become true, and I have no fears in the future. Nothing is more pitiful than I have lived with the V.C. and even in the refugee camp, in which the density of population is highest in the world with minimum sanitary conditions. So I won't be afraid anything will be come with me…Please remember me as one of your friends."

Honolulu Jan 27th 1980 – "I also attended an Engineering Review course at University of Hawaii at night … every day I come back home about 10pm. I now and feel tired but I'm happy…It's nonsense if you try to bring people together with their families but the countries in which they settle don't give them an opportunity to become good citizens. Most of them (just) end up as experts of carpet cleaning, car washing – even girls automatically become taxi girls. They tell their poor relatives still in Vietnam that they got good jobs such as in a building maintenance company… I hope to see you some day in USA. I fear that I'll become a depthless and without feeling because of American society."

Honolulu May 11 1980 – "I would like to inform you that I've just taken the Engineer-in-Training examination in the State of Hawaii. This is the first part of a professional examination. The exam was held 8 hours, the morning session consists of 150 questions and the afternoon session I had to solve 5 problems which had to cover at least four subjects. I have tried with all my effort but I really don't know what the result is. I forgot a lot of lessons that I had before 1973. ... I knew that I was the first Vietnamese civil engineer who registered in Hawaii."

Honolulu 7 August 1980 – *"I've passed the exam for registration of Engineer-in-Training in the State of Hawaii"*

Tampa 3 September 1980 – *"We have left Honolulu on 12/8/80 and arrived in Tampa City of Florida on 13/8/80. We missed Hawaii but we should leave because of too many reasons, especially my wife's relatives' troublemaking. I sent 26 resumes to 26 consulting engineer films in Tampa but up til now I've still no job. Meanwhile I've been waiting for an apt job, I was a dishwasher for a Chinese restaurant in Tampa. Every night I earned $25 plus about $2 tip. Just enough for the refugee life."*

Miami 7 January 1981 – *"Now, everything is OK for my family. I've worked as a project engineer. There are lots of Cubans here, most of them speak Spanish; therefore I had to learn some Spanish... I like to become a student rather than a worker, but I didn't have any opportunity... I hope you will be a businessman very soon. At this time I begin to study in order to take the professional engineer exam next November if I will be eligible.*

Miami 16 December 1981 – *"Since we took the risk down to here, it worked out good, at least better than in Honolulu, for the time being. But in the long run it's still nothing for the future. I also took the professional engineer exam last November and the result will be back in February. I hope I will pass. I plan to study the MS degree in Environmental after that... Miami, where most Vietnamese people are well established, some come here before 1975, lots came here since then. Most of them have good jobs. One owns a motel 24 units, one is Vice President for a hospital management company. Some work for Miami-based airlines as mechanics, some are computer analysts… I hope some day you will be here and my wife said that she cook some Vietnamese food for you and she think it should be better than Songkhla."*

I received what seems to have been a final letter some 3 years later, in August 1984, by which time I was back in Bangkok, in which he related that he had just bought a new house in Tampa, and was working as a senior consulting engineer, mainly in land development projects. He had worked out that to be really successful in the USA, he needed to have his own business, and so far had tried (and failed) with a couple of entrepreneurial ventures.

The third, Hoang Thi Le Thuy, was my final interpreter, and was still in the camp when I left Thailand, so our correspondence started even before she had left. A highly intelligent and cultured young girl, she spoke very good French and some English, claimed to be 16 years old (to be eligible for adoption as a minor) and in fact looked very young, but she seemed more mature, and never admitted what her real age was (I suspected 17 or 18). She had escaped with her younger brother, and on arrival in the camp they had quickly been "adopted" by the Millers, American Baptist husband and wife missionaries who lived in Songkhla and who arranged for her, as a minor, to be sponsored by and resettled with a Baptist family in Georgia.

Le Thuy was enrolled in High School for a year when she got to the US, and we corresponded for a couple of years afterwards. Her letters reflected her initial shock at being exposed to American culture and revealed a touching confusion and vulnerability as she entered adulthood and went on to University. As the letters suggest (again, translated from her excellent French), I became something of a mentor or elder brother for her.

Songkhla 28 August 1979 – "A huge thank you for your wonderful present (which was six Asterix books, in French) …There is no need to thank me for my interpreting duties – and furthermore not "invaluable", given that very often it was "free translation". I was very proud to fulfil this duty, added to which it was interesting to ask questions, play a bit at detective, and learn to observe people. Since your departure I have the feeling that I've been retired, I'm no longer the person-who-knows-everything-that-goes-on-in-the-camp, and I no longer recognise all the faces I meet."

Songkhla 25 September 1979 – "I got myself nomi-nated as "medical interpreter" by Doctor Bordes,[9] a rather pompous title, but in reality, work of little interest, since medicine is not fun at all – an opinion obviously not shared by the doctor. Anyway, you see how wise I am for my "10-z-?-z-years"? I haven't wasted my time and my medical knowledge reaches new heights….I will soon leave the camp, I think at the beginning of October."

Decatur 23 November 1979 – "My brother and are now settled quietly in the charming district of Decatur in Atlanta. I am, like the Vietnamese proverb, like a frog who's just escaped from its well, and I go from astonishment to astonishment. We now live with Mr. & Mrs. Tunnell and their son who's the same age as my brother. They work for the Home Mission Board to take care of the resettlement of refugees in the US. They speak a bit of Vietnamese, which

9. Dr. Bordes worked for Medecins Sans Frontiers and was assigned to the camp for a while.

is great help for my brother, and are simply wonderful people... I've been going to school since my second week in the US, and the education system is completely different from what I was used to."

Decatur 18 December 1979 – "Could I ask a big favour of you? I have to write a project for my history teacher, and I've chosen the UN as a subject. I have to base my work on primary and secondary sources, the primary sources have to be something real, concrete, like an interview or a newspaper article. So, in the end you are the only person who can fly to my rescue..." [I did send some documents]

Decatur 9 January 1980 – "I am now in a nest so cosy that more than ever I feel the significance of the slogan "they would like to have your problems", the meaning of which I asked you to explain for me in Songkhla...

"By the way, my research paper is now focussed on the question of refugees and the actions of the UN to deal with the problems, which – completely by chance – happens to

fall in your domain of expertise, so I wondered if I could ask you to share some of your professional secrets? The behaviour of American kids has shocked me a lot ... can you imagine a class in which the students jump on the table, chew gum, paint their lips, and even reply cheekily to the teacher?... But fortunately, not all are bad elements. I don't claim to judge the country that has opened its arms so hospitably to welcome me, I just note that I'm not yet used to what I'm seeing, because for now I'm having the same experience as Usbeck, Montesquieu's Persian."

Decatur 25 February 1980 – *"There are piles of things that astonish me, that I marvel at, that shock me, that I need to tell someone and if possible, ask for an explanation. I don't know if it's because I'm an adult that the world seems darker for me now, I am so disappointed the more I look into things in depth...*

"Some advice Mr. Lean, what do you think I could study at college? I would very much like your kind of work, as I haven't forgotten all that I came across in Vietnam and what I saw and heard in Thailand."

Decatur 22 March 1980 – *"I received an 'A' for my project and my teacher complimented me on the choice of subject and the good origin of my primary sources...*

"Could you give me your opinion on the current situation in Vietnam – what do you think will become of my country? I sometimes ask myself if I could be good at something for my compatriots. The irony is that I would never have had the "enthusiasm for dedication" but thanks to people like you, like the Millers, and Dr. Bordes.

"Mr. Lean, you said that my letters don't annoy you, but I fear that someone as busy as you will get tired of them. It's just that I have no-one to whom I can ask questions."

Decatur 13 April 1980 – *"...I would like my future to*

be linked to refugees somehow, and if possible be able to return to Vietnam (under the cover of the UN if Vietnam is still communist). Please advise me what I should study at college…"

Decatur 10 June 1980 – "…I'm on holiday and have just graduated from High School…"

Decatur 29 June 1980 – "…I've decided to opt for sociology, but I doubt that that will give me a speciality in anything. If I were to follow my personal interests, I would have studied literature, languages, painting, but for what end goal? I could not sit quietly beside the fire savouring the spiritual beauty of a work of art; I want to get involved in the agitations of the world, to feel that I am useful and competent in something."

Oklahoma 11 July 1980 – "At the beginning of the summer I was involved in interesting work, helping children from 7 to 12 years to learn English. They were from all over the world – Cambodia, Laos, Turkey, Iran. Now, I'm on a grand trip to the West crossing 15 states, camping at night. The family stopped at Oklahoma for a week, joining a church group. We study the Bible and do communal activities, and it's marvellous; the good intent, the candour, completely the opposite to communal activities of the communists, which are full of hypocrisy and mistrust."

Decatur 24 November 1980 – "…University life pleases me a lot. It's a private college, not very big, well enough known, the atmosphere is very intimate and rather puritan – I mean by that it is not too "yankee", not too "loose", which is far from displeasing to me given that I'm used to moderation. I still persist in the idea of studying political science but would like to be better prepared in terms of my use of English… But life itself is nasty. I'm bored because I feel useless, I find most people banal and uninteresting, and I need at least another 4 years before I can be qualified to do anything....You mentioned to me that you have a personal philosophy – is it that what helps you find life less nasty?"

Decatur 31 December 1980 – "I miss Asterix a lot. It's strange that the Americans read no French comics! Mr. Graham, tell me if you find the reflections of a young girl stupid; sometimes I get so depressed although I have no apparent reason. I can't express it to my parents in Vietnam, they have enough troubles of their own, I have to show them a happy image of myself. I certainly don't want to say – or rather show – anything to my adoptive parents, who might think I'm difficult or ungrateful, and I don't feel free to confide in them. It's completely absurd. Life is too difficult, and I'm the most absurd. Please put up with all this, it relieves me a bit to say it "out loud".

Decatur 30 January 1981 – "It's a great comfort to have someone to confide in. I find nothing bad in society, I've quite simply lost my North. I was thinking that all the world is bad, and it's not strangers who give you pain, it's often those on whom you count the most…When I was in Vietnam with the communists, there was no shortage of threats, hostility, and hypocrisy, but I didn't really feel it because I had my family as a fortress. It's a different world when you are alone. Caught off-guard, one finds oneself hypocritical and false, no better than others. All this reminds me of "The Power and the Glory" by Graham Greene … an illustration of all the evil around men, the worst being the evil within.

"But I have very interesting news to tell you. In February I will take a course in handling cameras, tape recorders and videotape machines, I'll therefore be able to learn the job of a reporter. My supervisor said that given my interesting adventure, it would be great to start with a report on my own experience…"

Decatur 1 August 1981 – *"I received your book, and had great pleasure in reading Narziss and Goldmund, just exactly what I need at the moment. Not everyone is lucky like Goldmund to have a Narziss to illuminate him. I sympathise with Goldmund when he has to face his true self... his life was simple before he had to face death, when he killed the robber, before he became conscious of his responsibility to live... We must continue to live and do our best to reconcile the angel and the beast.*

"I passed my exams at the end of the year, and after three days started my summer job, again helping immigrant children from 7 to 12 to learn English. I have complete freedom on everything I do, since it's a charity programme funded by a church... It's like this that I pass two thirds of my summer vacation, and in a month, I'll return to the routine of a student."

I have no further trace of correspondence from them, and I don't recall how or when our correspondence petered out, whether the letters stopped coming or whether I moved countries too quickly for them to catch up with me. After business school, I was in Thailand and Burma for a month, then back to the UK, and shortly afterwards in September 1981 was posted to the Philippines, returning home in March 1982. I then left the UN, so their letters may have got lost and the link broken.

I like to think that I always replied to the letters I received, and it may be that such relationships just have a limited lifespan. A natural conclusion, when the need or desire for a link with, or continuity between, a former existence and current life fades. The ending of the correspondence appeared to be a kind of graduation, almost a mutual recognition that it was time to let go.

10

Hong Kong interlude – April 1979

Despite the growing pressure of the situation in Thailand both at the border and on the coast, due to the shortage of staff I was asked to go up to Hong Kong to help the office there handle its growing burden of refugees from Vietnam. It was a good opportunity to change environment, and I checked into the old and very atmospheric Luk Kwok Hotel on Hong Kong Island (which had featured in the film "The World of Suzie Wong", but which has long since been rebuilt on more modern lines).

The brief Chinese invasion of Vietnam in February 1979 had intensified Vietnam's pressure on its Hoa population (ethnic Chinese who had settled in Vietnam). Many Hoa left by boat or crossed into China by land, and then made their way along the South China coast to embark on boats again to get into Hong Kong by sea. At around the same time both the Thai and Malaysian governments were trying to enforce a push-back policy, and Hong Kong became a more attractive destination (which it always was anyway when the SW monsoon was blowing). The Hong Kong government initially treated the arrivals as illegal immigrants, but soon came to an agreement with the UN to accept them on a temporary basis, pending resettlement.[10]

---

10. The UNHCR estimated that between 1975 and 2000, some 200,000 refugees from Vietnam arrived in Hong Kong, of whom around 143,000 were resettled overseas, and some 67,000 eventually repatriated. About 1,000 settled locally.

Shortly after arriving, I was asked by the UNHCR Representative, a charming but largely ineffective Singhalese, to attend a government reception on his behalf because (he said) he had a prior family commitment. So I turned up at Government House representing UNCHR, and was accosted by an official who demanded to know who the most senior UNHCR person there was. I admitted that I most closely fitted the description, whereupon he launched into a tirade about the UNHCR's sluggish and dilatory response towards a problem that was growing fast and was causing the Hong Kong Government increasing difficulties and expense.

It then dawned on me why my Singhalese colleague had been so keen for me to attend – he had anticipated what had been coming. I told the HK official that I was only on a temporary mission and that I would pass on the message, whereupon he became a lot friendlier and over several rounds of drinks, provided some insight into what was going on and what the Government's concerns were (the growing numbers, security issues, the escalating costs, and concern over long term solutions).

When I arrived in April 1979, the problem was building, but still relatively minor. The main centre where they were housed was at Sham Shui Po in Kowloon, and the first time I went there, no-one other than old and very young people were in the centre – all the others were out working. But as numbers began to increase, the Hong Kong government began to put more pressure on UNHCR to resettle them, eventually having to open new centres for them.

I was only there for a month to help streamline the interview process, but total arrivals for 1979 were estimated at over 68,000, with a further 100,000 arriving up to 2000. I was helped in the camp by volunteers from the Vietnamese community in Hong Kong – and again French became an essential tool, as the volunteer interpreter I worked with most often was Pierrette, a French-educated Vietnamese woman whose French husband was working in Hong Kong.

The office received word that some refugees were stuck in Macau, in those days still under the control of the Portuguese, who had rented it in 1554 from the Ming Dynasty rulers for trading purposes, before establishing a permanent settlement in 1557. It remained under Portuguese control until 1999.

Therefore, one morning I boarded the hydrofoil from a Hong Kong pier with an introduction to a Jesuit priest there, who met me at the Macau dockside in his white cassock, and immediately took me to a nearby café and ordered coffee and cognac for us both. Yet another interesting character and old Asia hand, he had been in Macau for decades, and like what little of the town I could see, he radiated a certain amount of mystery and intrigue. It was an overcast day and most of the dilapidated old buildings were green with mould.

We did a short tour on foot to sites where he said he thought some of the Vietnamese might be at that time of day, but none were to be found as they were all out working. He assured me that none of them were in any distress. Eventually we repaired to a restaurant near the harbour and had a long conversation over at least one bottle of wine before it was time to catch the hydrofoil back to the bright lights of Hong Kong.

It may have been an unproductive trip in terms of helping refugees but was a wonderful insight into a time and place that was rapidly fading into memory and was soon to be obliterated by modernisation and later by Chinese control. It was another place that I wish I had been able to visit in earlier days.

Four weeks in Hong Kong was enough to understand that the refugees were an irrelevant matter for the bulk of the population, and the expats I came across were usually surprised to hear that they even existed. They were far more focussed on earning their share of what Hong Kong was best known for – money.

So, having done my best to establish a more orderly system for interviewing and documenting the refugees, I flew back to Thailand and the mounting problems there.

11

Pressure on the borders

Thailand had recognised the Khmer Rouge government shortly after the fall of Phnom Penh in 1975, and had tried to establish a formal, if basic, relationship with the regime. At the same time, it was assisting the anti-KR opposition (called the Khmer Serei) that was scattered around the border area in different groups. When the KR crossed the border and attacked three Thai villages in January 1977, murdering men, women, and children, even that did not deter attempts to maintain official relations between the two countries.

The Khmer Rouge regime in Cambodia had also carried out deadly attacks on villages in both Thailand and particularly in Vietnam, where up to 30,000 people were reported to have been killed in repeated incursions into an area that had centuries before been part of the ancient Khmer empire and that the new KR communist government had stated it wanted to reclaim. Thailand and Vietnam had long been antagonists over Cambodia, and arguably, if it had not been for the arrival of the French in the nineteenth century, the country could have ended up being partitioned between the two. But having a buffer state between them was more beneficial to them both, and this dictated the geopolitical strategic dance that was to follow, conducted under the facade of the international humanitarian relief effort that began to build up in 1979.

In late 1978 the Vietnamese had had enough, and launched

a full-scale invasion of Cambodia, swiftly capturing most of the country and driving the Khmer Rouge and its captive population further west towards the Thai border, and into the Cardamom mountains in the southwest. China had been supporting the Khmer Rouge, and in February 1979, invaded the north of Vietnam to try and relieve the pressure on them. After fierce Vietnamese resistance, they pulled back after two months with heavy losses, having achieved very little, and Vietnam's occupation of Cambodia continued, where they set up a puppet government. As long as the Khmer Rouge regime was hostile to the Vietnamese, the Thai government was pre-pared to try to work with it, despite the border provocations, and after the invasion this became an even greater priority.

The Thais were opposed to the idea of having to accom-modate fleeing Cambodians, whom they called illegal im-migrants. By mid-April the Vietnamese offensive had pushed tens of thousands of KR and their followers to the Thai border. On 12 April 1979, despite protests from UNHCR, around 1,700 of the refugees from one of the older camps were rounded up, taken by bus and forced over the border into an area controlled by the Khmer Serei, who escorted them at gunpoint further into the interior.

Four days later, further attempts to force people back were interrupted by the UNHCR Field Officer on the spot, David Taylor, who had replaced David Jamieson. For that he was denounced by the Thai government for infringing Thai sovereignty, and when the UN Secretary General Kurt Waldheim visited Aranyaprathet on May 13th, Taylor was one of the relief officials who gave him a detailed briefing on the 12th April pushback. The Thais were embarrassed and infuriated, Taylor received death threats, and not long after-wards had to be withdrawn.

It was believed that numerous and frequent undocumented

push-backs of individuals and small groups had taken place along the border at this time. A report came in saying that on 16 April, in Buriram province to the northeast of Aranyaprathet, 826 Cambodians had been removed by the army from their temporary sites, taken further south, made to walk for two and a half hours and then pushed over a cliff. While this was uncorroborated, a much bigger incident occurred shortly afterwards that was widely reported.

In early June 1979, barely three weeks after Waldheim's visit to the camp, over several days the Thai military rounded up between 43,000 and 45,000 Cambodians from the Aranyaprathet area, bussed them round to the hilltop border at the temple of Khao Preah Vihear, and forced them back into Cambodia with almost no water and little food, down steep hills at the foot of which a minefield awaited them. Many died along in the process. All this occurred without any opposition from the agencies. It was reported in the international press, and the Thai government was reported as being pleased that it had gained the attention of the wider world. But it was a shameful and humiliating performance by everyone.

UNHCR did not replace David Taylor as Field Officer for some time, and at the end of July I was asked to visit the border area again to try and determine what was going on. I travelled along the border as close I could get to Cambodia while still staying on the Thai side, which was not straightforward, as the roads were just dirt tracks and there were no signposts. Along the road I could only find a few local Thai villagers, who all had different accounts of what they thought the situation was and where refugees might be.

The glaring absence of a Field Officer in the area had been raised in Bangkok and Geneva, and I reported to Goodyear after my trip that it was impossible to tell how many refugees there were, or what the Thais were doing to, or with, them. I

At work in a Cambodian camp with Khun Amorn, a key assistant.

repeated that there could be no hope of UNHCR being able to obtain a decent level of information, nor provide even a basic level of assistance or protection until and unless a new field officer were appointed to the area. In the meantime, the situation with the boat people in the south was not getting better.

Letter home 15 May 1979

Since I returned to Thailand we have all been submerged by the amount of work. While most of the headlines have been focussed on the extraordinary and pathetic exodus of Cambodians on the eastern frontier, the shores of southern Thailand are increasingly littered with the wrecks of fishing boats from Vietnam: a large one turned away from Songkhla went ashore further south and was immediately soaked in gasoline and fired. Rumours suggested that between 2 and 6 people weren't quick enough out of the hold.

The problems here, as you may have gathered, are now worse than ever (which is depressingly frustrating having worked my hide off for 3 and a half years and now face a graver problem that when I arrived) and I will just have to wait until a replacement is approved… The visit of Waldheim has helped to dramatize the plight of refugees here, so we are under more scrutiny than ever before: just at a time when the Thais have decided that enough is more than enough and are tuning people back across every border and at sea. Difficult to handle.

The uncertainty about the future has done marvellous things for my appreciation of life: senses become much sharper and each incident more involving.

Pin Yathay

Klong Yai is a small fishing village located on the thin finger of land that stretches down the southeast coast of Thailand, nestled in the shadow of the Cardamom Mountain range in Cambodia that marks the border between the two countries. The last village before the border post at Haad Lek, it was the physical limit of my range of responsibilities, and I used to visit from time to time to check whether any Cambodians had made it across the border.

Occasionally gunfire could be heard from Cambodia, and Khmer soldiers were sometimes to be seen on the top of the hills. I would call in at the police station, and one day in July 1977 the sergeant on duty told me that one man had arrived and was in the cells in the back. The cells were, in fact, just cages, and when I walked in, an emaciated frame in rags got up and asked if I could speak French. This was Pin Yathay.

An engineer who had studied in Canada under a government scholarship, he had been working at the Ministry of Public Works until the fall. He had lost his first wife and second child in childbirth, and he had married his first wife's sister, with whom he had two more sons. When the Khmer Rouge emptied Phnom Penh, he disguised his background, and was sent with his entire family of eight to work in countryside. Within two years most of them had died from malnutrition, overwork, or sickness, and when his identity was finally betrayed by an acquaintance, to avoid certain execution, he decided to flee with his wife over the Cardamom mountains. His sole surviving son was too ill to travel and had to be left behind, and his wife died along the way.

A garbled version of this spilled out of him in the Klong Yai police station, and I was able to arrange his transfer shortly afterwards to the Klong Yai refugee camp further up the coast. He gave me the name of a woman he had known previously in Phnom Penh, Yvette Pierpaoli, a livewire entrepreneur and humanitarian dynamo who lived in Bangkok, and who I had met and got to know through mutual friends. She was in regular touch with the Cambodian camps to see whether any of her friends from Phnom Penh had managed to get out, and her company ended up with a UN contract to supply rice to the camps.[11]

As soon as she found out that he had escaped she started the process that would see his eventual resettlement in France.

---

11. A colourful and friendly character, Yvette had run a trading company in Phnom Penh where she had lived until just before its fall and was said to have saved many Cambodians in the final days by flying them out in her chartered aircraft. At the same time, she was also rumoured to have preserved some ancient Khmer artefacts from falling into the hands of the Communists. John le Carré, who she had met in Phonm Penh in earlier days, and for whom she became a muse (and, widely believed, his lover), dedicated his novel "The Constant Gardener" to her. She left Thailand in 1985 to continue relief work in Mali, Niger, and Bangladesh, and was killed in a car accident in 1999 in Albania, while on a mission to assist refugees from Kosovo.

He subsequently wrote a couple of books about his experiences. The first, *"Murderous Utopia"* was published in French in 1980, and the second in 1987 *"Stay Alive my Son"*, a harrowing account of his family's suffering. He eventually remarried in France and had 3 more children.

12

The Storytellers
(Journalists and Reporters)

Refugees are an eternally appealing subject matter for journalists and reporters, providing endless human-interest material, and those in Thailand were no exception. The fact that they had fled from communism was a particular attraction for many journalists, especially those from the US, and the plight of the boat people became an increasing source of focus from the overseas press.

To a large extent this was necessary in drawing the world's attention to what was an on-going sore, and in putting pressure on Governments to accept refugees for resettlement. By and large, my relationships with journalists were good, especially those based in Bangkok, who knew the way things worked in Thailand and who were used to writing in ways that caused least offence. I joined the Foreign Correspondents Club (its clubhouse then located at the top of the Dusit Thani hotel), where it was possible to get a good meal or drink in an informal setting, and sometimes talk with any correspondents who were there.

An enduring problem was posed by those who wanted to visit the camp in order to uncover stories of hardship or abuse that would gain headlines. These certainly existed, but the Thais were acutely sensitive to any form of criticism, even if some of the stories were the result of their policies. One journalist who was a persistent nuisance was Henry Kamm, who wrote for the New York Times. He was the author of a couple of books about the region (one on Vietnam, one on Cambodia), and lived with Pham Lan Huong, a beautiful and extremely intelligent Vietnamese woman of Franco-Swiss nationality, who was working for the US immigration team.

Lan always came down to the camps with the US immigration teams, so I got to know her well, and very often Kamm would tag along to get access to the refugees in the camp and to sniff out stories that he would get published in the New York Times. In fact, he wrote well, and his articles eventually won him a Pulitzer Prize. To his credit he was one of the very few journalists who at the time wrote about the atrocities in Cambodia, but he didn't hesitate to call out or embarrass the Thais, or the UN, or the NGO's, whenever he could, in order to demonstrate what he clearly thought was his superior moral posture. He was often right.

I therefore had to spend quite some time dealing with such journalists, and the ripples that they caused, some of whom were just digging for dirt. I had no hesitation in challenging them on it, since the publication of their stories, often sensationalised, made my dealings with the local authorities that much more difficult. The Thais restricted access to the camps as much as they could, a policy partly driven by security concerns, and, no doubt, partly for fear of any embarrassing exposure. But now and again their policies led to disgraceful outcomes, and fully deserved to be exposed to the spotlight of international outrage. So we had to learn when, and how best, to work with the press; it was an uneasy and shifting balance of interests. Nonetheless, I was able to establish some good friendships with the Thailand-based members of the foreign press corps and could pass on – or selectively reveal – general information when asked. But never with any direct quotes or attributions.

Journalists were an inevitable part of the game, but I

learned much more from reporters, by which I mean journalists who had spent a long time in Asia and who had written books. They were mainly Americans, the successors of the eminent foreign correspondents (such as Dorothy Thompson and John Gunther) who had emerged as significant voices after the First World War in the wake of the Treaty of Versailles, at which the then President Woodrow Wilson had played such an overbearing part. They had access to and interviewed royalty, political leaders, and dictators, they mingled with European elites and literary figures, and had a powerful role in informing and shaping the attitudes of the American public to events in Europe, and also in influencing US foreign policy.

Ever since my arrival in Thailand at what was effectively the tail end of the Vietnam war, I had developed an unquenchable thirst to find out more about the war, the region, its history, and its peoples. During my first year, in Isan, one of the first genuine reporters I met through the US Consulate was Robert Shaplen, a correspondent for the New Yorker, who had had decades of working in Asia. He had been with Mao Zedong in Yunnan in 1946, in Indonesia during Sukarno's rise and fall, and had been in Saigon when it fell at the end of the war in 1975. He wrote many books on the region, one of which I subsequently read ("The Lost Revolution"), and he provided a rich historical perspective to what was going on.

A great source of education and inspiration for me, although I never met him, was Dennis Bloodworth, the former Far Eastern correspondent for the Observer newspaper. He had been posted to Saigon in 1954, became the first British journalist to be allowed into China (in 1955) after the Communist takeover, and wrote a number of entertaining books on China and the region (including an excellent book on Singapore's political evolution and the fight with the communists: *The Tiger and the Trojan Horse*). Most of the books were dedicated to his wife, who came from a prominent Peking family which had fled China. Soon after arriving in Thailand, I was advised (by an old Asia hand) to read his "An Eye for the Dragon: South-East Asia observed 1954-73", a brilliant book that gave me an invaluable insight into the politics of the region and a fascinating introduction to an area that was to become such a prominent feature of my life.

Another reporter I met was Anthony Paul, a Far Eastern specialist and roving editor of the Readers Digest magazine, who was based in Hong Kong. Paul had visited Cambodia as a war correspondent and was evacuated from Phnom Penh five days before its fall. An assignment took him to Guam to meet some of the Vietnamese who had escaped from Vietnam in April 1975, and there he came across a few Cambodians who were the first to relate the horrors of the Khmer Rouge regime. In September 1975, he visited the camp in Aranyaprathet to interview refugees, and subsequently returned a few times later that year when he came into contact with David Jamieson, and subsequently with me. He stayed in touch for a couple of years as we were able to give him news from the camps.[12]

In 1977 Paul and John Barron (another Readers Digest editor) published their book which in the United States was entitled *Murder of a Gentle Land. The Untold Story of Communist Genocide in Cambodia*. Another book, *Cambodia – Year Zero*, was also published in French in 1977, written by a French missionary, Francois Ponchaud, who had lived in Cambodia

---

12. In 1979, when I was stationed in Hong Kong for a month, Paul kindly invited me to dinner at his flat one evening, when he was entertaining Richard Nixon's cousin and family, who were on some kind of goodwill visit. It appeared to be the first time the family had been outside the USA, and they came across as a mixture of charm and credulity.

since 1965 and who had also been evacuated just before the fall of Phnom Penh. These were the first two books that described what was going on in Cambodia.

They were both denounced by leftist academics in the West who systematically downplayed reports of atrocities and propagated tales of a communist utopia. Noam Chomsky was one of the more prominent, quoted as calling Paul and Barron's book a "third rate propaganda tract." (When the evidence of Khmer Rouge excesses became undeniable, Chomsky, as a typically devious left wing academic, claimed he had never defended them, and tried to hide behind the excuse that the allegations were unproven and based on unverifiable sources).

Another leftist cheerleader for the regime was the British Marxist scholar Malcolm Caldwell, one its strongest foreign defenders. Ironically, in December 1978 the Khmer Rouge invited him and two Western journalists to visit Cambodia to witness the new ideological paradise. Shortly after having had a personal meeting with Pol Pot, he was murdered in his hotel bedroom in dubious circumstances. One of the two journalists who accompanied him, and who had taken refuge in her hotel bathroom when she heard the commotion from Caldwell's nearby room was Elizabeth Becker, an American who had been the Washington Post war correspondent in Cambodia, (and who also later wrote a book about the country, *When the War Was Over: Cambodia and the Khmer Rouge Revolution*).[13]

Among the journalists and writers who did eventually change their position on the Khmer Rouge was the controversial "anti-imperialist" Australian journalist and historian

13. I recall that we had dinner with Becker in Bangkok before she went into Cambodia with Caldwell, who may well also have been present at the dinner. There was a male seated at the far end of the table, but I don't think we spoke.

Wilfred Burchett. Burchett had been one of the first Western journalists to cover the devastation and radiation sickness of Hiroshima days after the dropping of the atomic bomb at the end of WW2. He subsequently reported on the Korean War, the Vietnam War, and the associated campaigns in Cambodia and Laos, often from behind "enemy lines," and his reporting was invariably seen as hostile to any anti-Communist narrative, for which he was even barred from entry to his native Australia.

Pol Pot had graduated from the University of Paris in 1953, where he had fallen under the influence of the works of Marx, Rousseau, Stalin, and Mao, as had many of the other future Khmer Rouge leaders who also studied in France. After WW2, French intellectuals had become entranced by Stalinism (as indeed had many of their British colleagues), and in the haunting words of Raymond Aaron in his 1955 book *The Opium of the Intellectuals*, they were people *"ready to tolerate the worst crimes as long as they are committed in the name of the proper doctrines."* As indeed were their Cambodian counterparts with such devastating and brutal effect twenty years later.

13

Camp Visitors

As I had mentioned in one of my letters home, the Field
Officers were often asked to meet and greet or take
care of overseas visitors to the camps. These people
varied greatly in quality, sincerity, and intelligence, ranging
from elected parliamentarians to staff from non-governmental
organisations and charities, academics, embassy political officers and military attaches, ambassadors and sometimes their
spouses, and even friends of the above.

> Lord Elton was on another visit here some time ago,
> and we were called in from the field to brief him. Utterly
> charming, he invited David Jamieson and I for dinner
> with him and we ended the evening listening to jazz in the
> Oriental Hotel.

Such visits might be for a couple of hours or several days, and
therefore the capacity for entertaining them, of necessity, had
to be flexible. It usually consisted of (at Songkhla) a seafood
dinner on the beach, or in town at a harbourside restaurant,
or (at Chantaburi) at a particular seafood restaurant at the
mouth of the Chantaburi river, just beside the jetty where the
daily catch came off the boats.

One of the more interesting visitors who I had to look after
and entertained for dinner at the Chantaburi restaurant was

a controversial American academic, George Kahin, a professor at Cornell University (where he had been the director of Cornell's Southeast Asia Program from 1961 until 1970). A recognised expert on Indonesia and apparently a prominent advocate for academic freedom, what I didn't know and had not been informed about, was that he had also been a leading critic of the Vietnam war, had been opposed to the US involvement there, was an early supporter of the Khmer Rouge, had tried to discredit stories of atrocities in Cambodia, and was involved in attempts to whitewash the regime.

For perhaps understandable reasons, the US Embassy ignored him when he turned up in Thailand to visit the camps, and he came down alone to Chantaburi for a couple of days. I took him to the camp, and we had a number of stimulating conversations, during which I made no secret of the horror stories I had heard from the Cambodians who had managed to escape from the country. He was extremely interesting, with a certain professorial charm as well.

It turned out that he had been a professor to Darryl Han, a Burmese colleague in UNHCR, who had earlier been posted in Hanoi, and who I knew slightly from Geneva. Darryl was one of the few more senior staff who had expressed any interest in my potential career with UNHCR and he had suggested that I study for a master's degree in political science at Cornell under Kahin, who had also suggested that I enrol at Cornell. I was seriously tempted with the idea and went so far as to arrange to sit the GMAT exam, but after my home leave in 1977, the workload in Thailand intensified further, and I decided to defer the notion of going back to study.

Not long after that, Darryl was killed in a car accident just outside the office in Geneva, which was a sad loss for UNHCR of talent and intelligence that it could ill afford. Without someone to encourage me in that direction, it also signalled the demise of my notions of pursuing further studies in the fields of development or humanitarian relief.[14]

Perhaps the most interesting, and certainly among the best company, of all the visitors to the camps was the author James Michener who, in the words of Britannica.com was a *"novelist and short-story writer who, perhaps more than any other single author, made foreign environments accessible to Americans through fiction. Best known for his novels, he wrote epic and detailed works classified as fictional documentaries".* He was already 80 when he visited Thailand, and I took him to the Laemsing camp where he met some of the refugees and a visiting Canadian Immigration team led by Ian Hamilton (in the foreground of the picture).

Michener was an orphan, had hitch-hiked round the US at the age of 14, and later won a scholarship to study at St. Andrews University. When he found out I was from Scotland, he admitted to being a life-long fan of Dundee United football club, which he had first gone to see play in 1931. He had walked across Scotland, ending up in the Western Isles, where he collected Hebridean folk stories, later studying art history in London and Siena. He briefly toured northern Spain with a troupe of bullfighters, and also worked on a Mediterranean cargo vessel. His method of writing was to carry out intensive research into the history of the country where his story was based. In the evening at the seafood restaurant on the river he entertained us all night until it closed, with many interesting stories.

---

14. The GMAT exam I had taken turned out to be of use a couple of years later when I applied to go to business school in France, and the modest score I had achieved was sufficient to reinforce the very unusual background that I presented, and that certainly differentiated me from other applicants.

The visit of immigration officials was always a popular event in the camps, and Ian Hamilton, who liked to walk around the camp, was invariably followed by a retinue of curious children

James Michener at Laemsing

JAMES A. MICHENER
BOX 125
PIPERSVILLE, PENNSYLVANIA 18947

March 6, 1978

Dear Mr. Lean:

    After a protracted trip I have returned home to
the heavy schedule of work that always seems to await
me, but I keep recalling vividly the experiences I
had in Thailand and the faces of the boat people I met
in the camps.

    One of the highlights of the trip was meeing you
at Chanthaburi and seeing a United Nations official at
work. You certainly have the high regard of all those
who come into contact with you; they felt you accom-
plished much.

    I send you my own warm wishes for success and
look forward to the day when the camps are emptied...
distant thought that time may be.

Sincerely,

James A. Michener

JAM no

Mr. Graham Lean
UNMCR
United Nations Building
Rajadamnoen Avenue
Bangkok, Thailand

When he got back to the USA, he had the courtesy to send a personal note of thanks, and when I left Thailand the following year on the way to a new position in Geneva, I travelled via Manila, Hawaii, and the USA, where I took the Amtrak Zephyr train from San Francisco to Chicago, and from there on to Washington DC. It was a 3-day journey, during which my companion guide was Michener's Centennial, his 1974 book that traces, from prehistory until the early 1970's, the story of the plains of northeast Colorado, through which the train passed.

14

Practical implications

The rate of new arrivals fluctuated with the season, more arriving during the northeast monsoon which lasts from April/May to October/November, blowing on to the eastern coasts of southern Thailand and Malaysia, while fewer came during the reverse southwest monsoon. The system that had been set up in agreement with the Ministry of Interior required that provincial offices submit budgets to provide for the existing refugees in camps.

So when arrivals increased, there was little or no flexibility in how the provincial authorities could react, no spare funds to cater for them, and the danger of the boats being sent back to sea intensified. At the same time, the lack of resources weakened any argument I might offer that the refugees should be allowed to stay on moral or humanitarian grounds.

A further problem was that there was only one camp in the south, in Songkhla province, and while authorities in other provinces along the coast were happy to send any new arrivals over to Songkhla, they had to get permission from Bangkok to do so, and as more than one governor argued, it was difficult to argue that they should help Vietnamese when they didn't have any budget to help the poorer Thais in their provinces, most of whom in the southern provinces were Moslem.

I therefore reached an agreement with the office in Bangkok that whenever I heard about a group of new arrivals,

I could ask for funds to be sent to a local bank, from which I would draw out cash to buy essential emergency supplies. The system was completely based on trust (I would get a merchant in the local market to sign a paper listing the supplies I had bought) and worked out very well, its speed and flexibility being the key factors. With the invaluable help of Surat, we got to be quite well known (and welcomed) in the market as each time I would pay cash (up to US$2,000 in Thai Baht) on blankets, rice, tinned food, tarpaulins, fish, vegetables, and toiletries.

The Vietnamese were sometimes to be found on a beach, or in the grounds of a temple or a school, and since they had usually been robbed several times, were usually destitute, and therefore very grateful for what we brought them. In most cases the areas they arrived at were poverty-stricken, and in order to try and avoid the locals stealing what we brought (which did happen), I always sent Surat round to the local village to present the village chief with a share of the goods as a goodwill gesture and to reduce the risk of such theft. Of course, this aspect of the relief was not reported officially to Bangkok, although Saowanee, the finance chief, was well aware of what was going on.

Such direct assistance activities cost very little and became an essential part of the game. It cost the local authorities nothing, meant that they could not be accused of helping Vietnamese at the expense of the poorest locals, and occasionally allowed them to be more lenient in terms of interpreting whatever policy was emanating from Bangkok.[15] But above

---

15. The official position of the Thai Government fluctuated between grudging toleration of the agreed co-operation with the UN, and from time to time, out-right rejection of any temporary asylum policy, depending on the message it wanted to send to either the Vietnamese Government or to prospective refugees, to the US Government, to the UN, or to all of them.

all, apart from the immediate material relief, it bought time for the new arrivals to be interviewed, and accelerated their transfer to the relative safety of the camp.

On one such occasion, a boatload of Vietnamese had landed in Pattani province after being attacked en route and had been towed out again. They had then been attacked again, but managed to get back to land, where they damaged their boat sufficiently so they could not be sent away a second time. By the time I had heard about them and driven down to Pattani, they had been brought to a shed not far from the provincial office, where I met the Governor.

I asked to be given access to group, and for permission to bring them some necessities, and promised to interview every family for resettlement. He granted both requests, but with the customary threats of having them sent back out to sea again. I went off to conduct the interviews, while Surat headed to the market for supplies.

The refugees were exhausted, terrified, and weak from hunger and fear. One middle-aged man, a former civil servant in South Vietnam who spoke English well, had completely lost his emotional control – tears were pouring down his face, he was dribbling from nose and mouth, and he implored me to take his young daughter away with me to save her life. It was all I could do to calm him down and reassure him that he and the family would be safe, and that I would arrange for their transfer to the camp in Songkhla.

Some of the others who had been through the same experience were impressively stoic throughout the whole episode and helped to calm him down. I completed all the interviews, managed to get a message through to Bangkok, and Surat came back with the essential supplies. Before leaving, I went back to see the Governor and asked him to ensure that the group was kept securely until he received clearance to move

them to the camp in Songkhla, which occurred a few days later.

When I started working with the refugees, I was moved and often deeply shaken by some of the stories I heard, but in order to be able to function effectively I had had to learn to detach from any kind of emotional involvement in whatever immediate situation or individual case I encountered. I quickly realised that trying to appeal to a Thai official's humanitarian instinct was a waste of time. It was not that they were void of empathy, but they seemed not to be able to extend it to the Vietnamese (very much the "other"), who they distrusted, disliked, and feared.

My dealings with any official therefore became more coldly transactional. They were faced with a local problem; I represented the most immediate and probably the best temporary solution available, even if it still meant that they were going to be inconvenienced by administrative duties reporting to Bangkok, or by diverting police resources to oversee the refugees. Hence, they were always tempted and quite happy simply to remove the problem whenever it appeared by sending the boats out again to go on to Malaysia.

During the three years I was roving the coastline of Thailand, I never "lost" any group that I was able to be in contact with. By this I mean that all the refugees I met outside the camps were subsequently transferred into the camps and eventually resettled. But what I never knew, nor indeed could know, was how many may have arrived and been sent out again before the news could get to me.

15

Mission to Koh Samui

T he missionaries were ever-present in and around the camps, and they could be and often were very helpful in terms of providing emergency assistance or being a conduit for information between the camp and the Vietnamese community in the USA. They could also inadvertently cause a lot of trouble with the ever-sensitive Thai authorities by over-reacting emotionally to events, or by complaining about things that they thought should have been done but hadn't. Since they were in regular contact with the US Consulate, invariably their complaints would get back to the Bangkok office or to the US Embassy. They were an effective, if sometimes annoying, pressure group.

In June 1979, I received reports through the missionary network that a group of Vietnamese had been detained for some months on Koh Samui. I was advised to make contact with a Father Joseph there, and so headed up to Surat Thani one morning to catch the ferry over to the island to investigate. The following narrative is from notes I wrote at the time:

We arrived into Surat Thani to be told that the ferry to Samui had already left, but we made it with 15 minutes to spare, and I left the driver to wait for my return. I was allocated seat no.9 up at the front port side of the crowded boat, seated beside the Pooyaiban (head) of a village to the south of Surat. Seated in front of me was a group of policemen with carbines, apparently guarding a payroll of 1m+ Baht. The ferry was a "cigar boat", a long tube with a shallow keel, ideal for calm inshore waters which were the norm in that area.

We cast off at 12.30 in sunny weather, but dark clouds were building from the West, and a storm hit us at around 14.00, very strong winds, rain, and heavy seas which gradually worsened. Our direction was approximately ENE, so the wind was coming directly into our port beam. The pilot was finally forced to reduce speed, leaving us more exposed to the increasingly heavy waves which crashed alarmingly into the side, making the boat yaw and teeter from one wave crest into the next trough, and then up again. At about 14.30 the reality became apparent. What had until then been a heavy storm viewed, slightly dreamily, through the tinted perspex windows, became, as we slid down into the full force of the next wave, in an instant a torrent of water that smashed through the window I was seated beside, drenching me, the Puyaiban, and the policemen.

There were screams, and the next half hour saw the level of panic inside the boat rise gradually – another crash of water was followed by further screams from the back of the boat, anxious faces staring forward, and some of the people behind trying to move forward only stopped by some of the police and the pilot shouting for everyone to be calm and stay in their seats. We limped on, the tension worsened by the knowledge that two weeks before a similar boat had been caught in a storm in the same waters and had overturned apparently because the passengers had panicked, drowning at least 10 people.

The jetty in Koh Samui is on the West of the island, a long finger with a T-shape at the end, ideally positioned against the prevailing NE monsoon winds, but this storm was blowing hard from roughly a WSW direction, and therefore directly towards the shore. At around 15.00 the boat edged into the marginally calmer waters behind one of the T-shape structures; this helped to break the waves somewhat, but as we were in danger of being driven on to the pier, for the next hour the boat remained beam on to the waves, which crashed through the broken windows with increasing frequency, each time sending a shudder through the vessel and visibly heightening the tension on board.

An hour later, after unsuccessful attempts to avoid ropes that were mooring a large fishing boat against the pier, the ferry was finally swung around and attached to the underside of the T part of the pier. Throughout the hour-long broadside we had endured, two Buddhist monks had been the only ones to try and maintain order, one shouting that he had with him a valuable amulet that would guarantee everyone's safety, but as soon as relative calm was established, both monks swung themselves overboard and were picked up by people on the pier. A large crowd had gathered there as we were being battered by the storm, and our struggles beyond the pier and our attempts to dock had been watched (and clearly enjoyed) by a large audience, who cheered anyone who decided to use the rope to pull themselves to land, groaned or laughed each time an especially large wave caved in another window, but who otherwise had no clue what to do to help. I remember clearly looking up at the faces on the pier above that were looking down and realising with horror that they were really only there for the spectacle, to see what would happen.

Eventually the sea calmed a bit, the tide started to drop, and a few passengers managed to scramble off the back of the boat when it drifted close enough to the moored fishing boat. At that point I noticed a small figure in a white cassock striding along the pier, waving his arms and shouting at people to bring up one of the smaller boats beached nearby to the aft of the ferry so people could disembark. Someone (possibly me) had raised this idea on board, with one of the passengers, an engineer, suggesting that the ferry company didn't want to waste money hiring boats to make a rescue.

A rise in the volume of noise in the cabin betrayed increasing distress, the police sergeant threw up out of a broken window, as did a police lieutenant through another. Panic in the boat intensified, and it was lucky that by then an open boat had been brought up to the back of the ferry and so the ensuing rush to get off could be coped with reasonably well. Finally, around 17.00, one of the last 4 or 5 passengers, after a crouched shuffle through the upper cabin window, I climbed out, wet, shaken, wobbly on my legs, and very, very glad to be back on land.

Father Joseph (for it was he) saw me and immediately came over to introduce himself, asked where I was staying, and as I had not booked anywhere, said he would put me up in the mission. He had a small moped, just big enough to take my extra weight sitting on the back clutching his waist, and we headed back to his house. He shouted over his shoulder that it was the worst storm for 6 months, and that it had knocked out the electricity on the island.

At the mission Father Joseph showed me to a small, spotlessly clean room with a crucifix on the wall, and because I had told him that I was from Scotland, then brought me a very welcome cup of hot tea. He put the cup down, fished under his cassock and – as if by miracle – produced a half bottle of whisky, out of which he tipped a generous amount into my tea, saying that it would warm me up. It did."

Father Joseph was a diminutive Italian Jesuit, who must have been around 70 years old at the time. He told me that he had lived in Thailand for around 50 years, since leaving his seminary aged only 19. He spoke Thai fluently, as well as both the Northeast (Isan) and Southern dialects. That evening after supper he invited me to sit in on an informal catechism he gave (in their own dialect) to an illiterate family from the Northeast who were staying at the mission, telling stories illustrated with paintings of Jesus and other religious figures. It was both touching and sincere. I slept extremely well that night.

Next morning, we talked about my reason for being there. He thought there were no longer any refugees on the island – a few had arrived some months before and had stayed for a while but were then moved to the mainland. He agreed to take me to the police station to ask there, and then to see his clinic. We set out on his moped again, promptly had a puncture in the rear tyre, and had to walk a mile into the village to get it repaired. That took time, and when it was fixed, we departed again at high speed, his cassock flapping around our legs, only for him to realise that he had dropped his keys at the garage. Back we went again at equally high speed, found the keys, and eventually arrived at the clinic, which was a basic but friendly and seemingly efficient place that catered for the local community.

We later called in at the police station, where he seemed to be well known, and were duly told that his information about Vietnamese had been correct. That evening we had a long talk over the state of the world, about which he seemed to be very well informed. He had an Old Testament view of the moral climate of the age; it was bad ("les débauchés" of Hollywood were identified in particular), getting worse, and mankind could not continue in the same Sodom and Gomorrah vein.

He struck me as a very genuine, compassionate, and humble Christian, and I developed a great affection and respect for him in the short time I was with him. He dropped me off at the ferry on his moped early the following morning, and sped off again, cassock billowing behind him. I climbed into another metal tube and returned to the mainland across a millpond flat sea. I never returned to Samui and never saw him again.

16

More politics

At the end of June 1979, the member states of the Association of Southeast Asian Nations (ASEAN), in a rare statement of co-ordinated solidarity, announced that they would not accept any new arrivals from Vietnam. The pushbacks that had been occurring now became official policy, and the whole notion of temporary asylum was at risk across the region.

A month later, in July, the UN Secretary General convened an international conference on Indochinese refugees in Geneva, stating that "a grave crisis exists in Southeast Asia for hundreds of thousands of refugees." By then some 350,000 Vietnamese were stuck in camps around the region, mainly in Malaysia and Hong Kong, but in other countries as well. The Malaysians and Thais were the most active and vocal in their opposition to the Vietnamese exodus, and in their efforts to push back the boats.

The result of the conference was a doubling of resettlement pledges (to 260,000); Vietnam, under intense pressure from the USA, finally agreed to approve a programme of "orderly departures" direct from Vietnam for (mainly) cases of family reunion; while Indonesia and the Philippines agreed to establish regional resettlement processing centres to handle the growing numbers, and to enable refugees to be taken sooner from the countries where they had first arrived and had been put into camps.

This was the result of an increasingly established pattern of informal emigration from Vietnam, which over the course of a few years had become more organised, cynical, and business-like (run by people-smuggling syndicates). Private initiatives were still being organised, but the Vietnamese had quickly worked out that there was money to be made from those who wanted to leave.

The earlier boat arrivals (in 1975-6) generally had better, or luckier, or at least less risky, escapes than those coming later, which were increasingly subject to attacks by fishing boats, mainly Thai, but of other nationalities as well. Not all the Thai boats were predatory, as the statement by one group upon reaching the safety of the camp reflects (see Appendix 1), but very many were. And as time passed and the flow of arrivals increased, so too did the violence. At first it was robbery for gold, jewels, and US dollars that in the early days some boats certainly carried and that led to the rumour spreading throughout the fishing communities that Vietnamese boats were rich – and easy – pickings.

One time in Songkhla in early 1976 a recently arrived group asked if they could get permission to go back to their boat to retrieve something they had left in it. They claimed that in Vietnam, before leaving, having heard of the risk of robberies at sea, they had had some gold fashioned into a shape that looked like a piece of the engine, and to hide it, had attached it to the real engine and covered it with oil and dirt. They had had to abandon it when they were taken to the camp and had intended to go back to retrieve it. The Thai police sergeant in charge of the camp was brought into the venture and one evening drove a couple of the Vietnamese up the coast to where they had landed. But while the boat was still there, the locals had stripped it of everything, including the engine.

But such riches were not widespread, and largely petered out as more sophisticated methods of paying for escape became more common. The attacks were then increasingly directed towards the people (robbery and assault), and the abduction and rapes of the younger women became more common.

The official UNHCR history of the period states that in 1977, around 15,000 Vietnamese arrived in Southeast Asian countries, but by the end of 1978, there were there were nearly 62,000 Vietnamese 'boat people' in camps throughout Southeast Asia, including Hong Kong and Malaysia where the bulk were to be found. The rate of departures from Vietnam kept increasing, in large part attracted by the well-established resettlement programmes that were in operation, led by the US Government. And the exodus increased significantly in 1979, with more than 54,000 new arrivals recorded in June of that year alone. Pushbacks of boats became increasingly routine, and the official UNHCR history blandly states that: "*As the numbers of arrivals grew, so too did local hostility*".

By this time some of the departures from Vietnam had become more blatant commercial enterprises, and the arrival off Malaysia in November 1978 of the Hai Hong, a steel hulled freighter carrying around 2,000 people revealed the extent to which people smugglers had become active. UNHCR pushed for them all to be regarded as refugees, and when this was accepted by Malaysia on the understanding that they would all be resettled, the business model was proven.[16]

Apart from such larger boats organised by what would today be called "people smugglers", escapes were still being

---

16. Appendix 2 is a copy of a summary position statement (in my view accurate), prepared in 1980 by the US Consulate and the Embassy refugee section that analyses why people were still leaving Vietnam.

made by enterprising and daring individuals. One of the most remarkable was a group of 6 men who had built a raft with 30 bamboo poles and 5 oil drums and had paddled their way over the Gulf to land in front of the camp on 9 June 1979. I was sceptical, but their story was thoroughly checked by the refugees in the camp, who verified it.

By this time a new camp had been constructed in front of a beach area to the south of the town. The initial facility that had grown up opposite the police station in town had become overwhelmed with the numbers of new arrivals, and there was no more space available. The boats the Vietnamese had arrived in were cluttering up shoreline, rotting away as they were plundered for materials for shelter or fuel, and the patience of the local community was wearing thin. The Provincial Governor therefore recommended that a new camp be built, well out of sight, and this was opened in December 1978. Some 3,000 people were moved in, and by the time I left the following year, the number had grown to 6,000.

The smaller boats continued to arrive, most with stories

of great hardship and pirate attacks, and the level of hostility mentioned in the UNHCR history ebbed and flowed depending, in Thailand at least, to a large extent on the volatile background geopolitics. At any given time, this influenced the message that Bangkok wanted to send to Vietnam (both to the government and to any would-be refugees), to the UN, and to the countries of resettlement, especially the USA.

The attitude towards refugees in Bangkok was interpreted in the provinces in varying degrees of indifference or enthusiasm, and of course, the official attitude of hostility towards the Vietnamese in particular seemed to spur the fishing community to keep up its unpunished attacks on refugee boats, as if they interpreted their actions as patriots defending the Thai nation.

We also had to deal with the occasional group of Vietnamese who had been picked up at sea by passing freighters. Maritime custom dictates that any ship coming across another vessel in distress on the high seas should provide assistance, and therefore commercial sea traffic in the area inevitably would cross the paths of boats making the run from Vietnam. Many new arrivals recounted how they had seen freighters that had ignored them, but occasionally there were genuine rescues, such as when an escaping boat was in danger of sinking or had been wrecked. But any rescue at sea had major implications for the owners of the vessels. The people rescued had to be let off the ship somewhere, but most countries in the region did not want to encourage this kind of activity, and so generally refused to let them disembark without a guarantee of resettlement from the government of the country in which the boat was registered.

Any delay in port was expensive for boat owners, who were under (commercial) pressure to drop off or pick up their cargoes as quickly as possible. On one such occasion, the

M.V. Toledo, en route to Bangkok, had rescued a boatload of Vietnamese and had arrived at the Klong Toey port where, of course, the Thai Immigration officials refused to let them off the boat. A message at high level went to Geneva, which then instructed us to interview them as quickly as possible. Since Jacques Mouchet was visiting the Bangkok office at the time, he, plus the young Finnish protection officer, accompanied me to conduct the interviews. Either the Danish or Norwegian Government provided a guarantee of resettlement, and the group were allowed to disembark to be lodged temporarily in the Bangkok immigration gaol before being flown out.

The Americans

The US Consulate in Songkhla was a regular port of call to share information, and I got to know the consuls and other officials there quite well. We would regularly play golf on the unkempt 9-hole course in front of the Samila Hotel, have dinner together, or sometimes head off to Haad Yai in the evening for entertainment. The consulate usually steered its refugee-focussed visitors to me for informal briefing, so there was a steady flow of journalists, retired or active State Department officials, diplomats from the Bangkok Embassy, or other visitors from the USA, many of whom ended up at the Seven Sisters for dinner.

I found the US foreign service people I came across both professional and intelligent, and it was easy to make friends. Many of them had served in Vietnam during the war, either in the military or with the State Department, and so were very knowledgeable and always ready to share their stories. They also, in a self-interested way, tried to be as helpful as they could, reporting to the Bangkok Embassy on events in the camp, problems with the Thais, the rate of new arrivals, and any other issue that arose. They could also occasionally cause problems by interfering (sometimes unnecessarily in my view), by inflating an issue that I thought could be better handled discreetly, or sometimes by listening too closely to what the missionaries were telling them. Overall, it was a good relationship that worked well, and without any doubt, from my local perspective their generally supportive influence greatly strengthened UNHCR's standing in the eyes of the Thai authorities.

I would also on occasion run into other kinds of Americans with very different backgrounds, usually in particular bars in Bangkok, who were often willing to talk about what they had been up to in Laos or Cambodia or Vietnam, and from these conversations I learned a lot about their personal stories, recent history, Asia, corruption, or vice; the sort of things that journalists often knew about but tended not to report on.

17

A final incident

B y mid-1979, the time for my departure was finally nearing. Two new Field Officers were sent out to take over from me. Koichi Koizumi was a Japanese JPO (Junior Professional Officer), seconded from the Japanese Ministry of Foreign Affairs; Theodore "Ted" Schweitzer III was, clearly, American. Highly intelligent, he had studied languages at university in Iowa, had trained as a teacher, and first arrived in Thailand in 1974 to work as a teacher and librarian. He was married to Wanna, a Thai woman, had a young daughter, and spoke Thai very well.

Their introduction to the scene could not have been more dramatic. Shortly after arriving in Songkhla, we received word that a boat had arrived in Songkhla itself. Unfortunately, it had the misfortune to approach the beach in front of the Marine Police headquarters. The story that emerged was that the marines had tried to warn them off by firing in the air, but as they got closer to the beach one of the troopers fired his carbine directly into the tightly packed boat, killing two men with a single round.

By the time we got round there, the beach was crowded with locals, and a Thai patrol boat had already fixed a tow to the refugee boat and was moving to pull it out to sea. The deck was crammed with refugees, crying for help with their arms above their heads in supplication, the two dead men hanging upside down from the side of the boat.

I left Koichi and Ted on the beach and since I knew the Governor was away in Bangkok, raced round to the Deputy Governor's house. I found him loading his clubs into his car, about to leave to play golf, and he said that he had no authority over the military, and that I would have to contact Bangkok. At the telephone exchange I managed to get a call through to the office quite quickly, reported the situation, and headed back to the beach to find a visibly shaken pair of new Field Officers watching as the boat was being towed out to sea.

The next day we heard that the boat had succeeded in making land further south, but only after being attacked again by fishing boats after the marine police boat had left it outside the 20-mile coastal territorial limit. After making it back to shore, the Vietnamese had damaged their boat beyond repair. What exactly happened to them after that I never found out, but the local authorities moved them to the Songkhla camp shortly afterwards.

But I was glad to be moving on, even if it appeared (and in fact turned out to be the case) that the situation was getting worse rather than better. I had been on the ground for four years, which was quite long for a field posting, and while I felt I was getting increasingly effective in doing the job and dealing with the situations that arose, (essentially, a series of crises),

Farewell party in Songkhla
Koichi Koizumi, Ted Schweitzer, Wanna Schweitzer, GL

I was at the point where what was later called "compassion fatigue" had set in.

The work had become an increasingly repetitive routine, I was getting tired of the constant movement (I rarely spent more than 3-4 days in any one place for a period of about 3 years), I was becoming increasingly cynical of the background politics, and had had enough of the Thais' attitude and their grudging and limited co-operation. I had therefore welcomed the offer of a position as Desk Officer in Geneva for the un-folding Cambodian programme and was looking forward to the change of scene and tempo.

18

Geneva revisited

The city hadn't really changed much in my absence, but I certainly had, and the number of boat arrivals in Thailand had continued to increase since my departure. Against a background of intensified hostility by the Thai Government towards all the refugees either present in, or arriving on, their territory, the ferocity of the attacks on the boats varied in intensity – eye-witness reports started to accumulate, recording that in some cases boats were deliberately rammed and sunk, young women were raped multiple times, some being taken off the boats, handed on from fishing boat to fishing boat, and then thrown in the sea when they had outlived their usefulness and to avoid detection.

My replacement as Field Officer, Ted Schweitzer, became renowned for his actions in saving Vietnamese who had been marooned on Koh Kra, an uninhabited island about 30 miles from the Thai coast. Fishermen/pirates sometimes towed entire boatloads of refugees to Koh Kra, robbing any valuables they could find and selecting women to rape. They would then alert other fishing boats would come by so the crews could take turns with the women. There were many grim stories from survivors, and Ted personally rescued over 1,200 refugees from the island. In a personal letter to me in early 1980, he described what he had been up to.

Songkhla 19 Jan 1980 – "I don't know if you know how one of these rescue attempts takes place, so I'll tell you a little. I have some informants (among them were the crews of helicopters that serviced the gas rigs in the Gulf of Siam) who tell me of refugees on the island. I then go to Pakpanang, rent a fishing boat, and with Thai police, marine police and the district officer, set off for Koh Kra. Eight hours later we arrive, anchor about 500 metres offshore, and I swim in. I then gather up the refugees, send those men who can swim off to the boat; those who can't swim, I swim out with them one by one. Back and forth, it's difficult and dangerous. This is why I'm going to Singapore to buy life-saving equipment.

"The stories these people tell are worse than you have read. I've been there 5 times now and just about didn't make it back last time. The last time we got there about 23.00 and an attack was in progress – I could hear screams from where I was on the boat. The police never swim ashore with me, and I knew they wouldn't this time either. But I had to go; I waited about 10 minutes, and I just had to go even knowing it was suicide. I eventually stopped the raping and promised the pirates not to identify them if they didn't kill me – which they wanted to do. They left after beating me, but they didn't shoot. I have over 100 cuts and bruises and 15 stitches, but none of the refugees was killed.

"The next morning, I was feeling OK and the rescue took place with no loss of life at about 7.30, despite the very heavy seas. However, on the way back to Pakpanang our rescue boat was attacked by seven pirates, but thanks to Sgt Kim, a Thai policeman, he talked them out of further violence. We have identified 3 pirate boats from this latest attack on the island and I have received renewed threats. On the way back to Pakpanang I was lying on the deck of the boat half dead and a refugee girl lying beside me, who speaks

French, crying, said "Can't someone do something about this island?" She lost her husband, daughter, brother and mother in the attack. I promised her we would do something about it. I hope you can help me keep my promise, Graham. I have seen too many deaths and rapes there for me to leave before I fulfil my promise to that girl. I'm enclosing for your information, an open letter from one of her friends who was on the same boat.

"If I don't get killed here, and if the Thais don't kick me out of Thailand, when I get this job done, I want to work in a post where I can help with a permanent solution to the Vietnamese problem, perhaps the family reunion scheme. I'm sorry to write such a serious personal letter but I'm up to my neck in trouble and worry for these people here. It's impossible to face the question of how many there were in the past that we don't know about. And how many are still to come? I feel that our work has just begun here, and I'm almost worn out already. The murder, rape and cruelty begin to make their imprint on me. Mr. Rizvi wants me to set up the Songkhla office and move on, and I can't complain about that. It's just that I want to be sure someone who really cares will take over.

"Mt Koizumi is now in charge of "camp operations" and doing quite well. He's an organised methodical worker and I think it was a mistake to have originally put him on the beach – such a messy, unorganised place. Really, he's doing OK as long as my computer controls his guidance system… Surat now has a regular UN contract and we still rent his car also. He's a great help, officially and personally."

He added that his wife, who had been three months pregnant at the time, had suffered a miscarriage when she saw the state he was in.

Songkhla 15 March 1980 – "I don't know whether to thank you or curse you! As you probably know I've had nothing but interested parties hounding me since I last wrote you. For the life of me I can't remember exactly what I wrote – it would be interesting to see! I recall that I had just returned from the island from a night mission, but that's about all.[17]

"We just assisted in the arrest of 13 pirates and 5 police-men in Surat Thani and assisted in the release of 16 girls (refugees) held in a brothel in Songkhla. At the time of the "bust", the background work done by me, we were elated at having rescued the girls. The pimps tried to kill them all to prevent testimony. However, after the rescue we found out that the policemen who carried out the bust also screwed the girls at the time. I suppose it doesn't matter, one more or less, but I am continually slapped in the face by reality. After all I've seen in 38 years one would think me unshocka-ble, but I assure you I'm not. Anyway, nothing was said, and only the ones who sold the girls were arrested. We now have 6,000 in the camp, and 1,000 on the beach, so we're busy".

Songkhla 29 October 1980 – "… Things here seem worse with you gone and not providing moral support… Piracy is continuing to escalate with over 70% of the boats now arriving having been attacked numerous times."

Ted (photographed overleaf in happier times) left Songkhla after a year of such recklessly brave actions which far exceeded the normal call of duty for a UN official. He left UNHCR shortly thereafter, apparently on medical grounds, and returned to

---

17. When I received Ted's letter I had circulated it within the office with the letter he had enclosed from the Vietnamese woman he had mentioned. It provoked the reaction I had hoped it would, hence his reference to the interested parties that sought him out subsequently.

the USA where in 1982 he set up a charity called the S.E. Asia Rescue Foundation, which according to its website provides "emergency food supplies, medical care and shelter to refugees, displaced persons and other needy and oppressed people in Southeast Asia, Northeast Asia and elsewhere as needed". Subsequently, he somehow managed to get into North Korea to provide assistance there.

A website was set up by Vietnamese former refugees that describes some of the incidents that occurred on Koh Kra. It is disturbing and shocking in equal measure, and not for the fainthearted. An extract from the site (https://refugeecamps. net/Kohkraintro.html) reads:

Until spring of 1981, Thai fishermen hunted refugee women on that island. According to UNHCR, one female refugee was severely burned when southern Thai fishermen, attempting to flush her out, set fire to the hillside where she was hiding. Another cowered for days in a cave, waist deep in water, until crabs had torn the skin and much of the flesh away from her legs. By Oct 1980, 160 refugees are known to have died on that island alone. The total no doubt was far higher before a detail of six or eight marines was stationed on the island in the spring of 1981 and halted the carnage. On April 2012 we arrived to Kok Kra to install a plaque. The engraving on the plaque reads:

"In honor of the thousands of Vietnamese refugees who were marooned, abused, tortured, and even murdered here on Koh Kra Island. May their suffering never be forgotten. With heartfelt thanks to Mr. Ted Schweitzer, who was instrumental in saving thousands of marooned refugees."

19

Moving on

When I got back to Geneva, Jacques Mouchet and his family (his wife Somjit, and young daughter and son) very kindly offered me a room in their apartment in Annemasse (just across the border in France) until I got settled, and so I was able to enjoy a small extension of Asia which helped my readjustment. It was a very enjoyable period, with great memories of trying out ski-de-fond under Jacques' instruction and having lunch with some of his relatives who lived in a village high up in Haut Savoie. After three months, I finally bought a car, a white Alfa Romeo Alfasud Sprint, and moved into a small, unfurnished studio that belonged to David Jamieson in Ferney-Voltaire in France, located just over the border to the north of Geneva. I bought a bed and a bookcase. And I was restless.

If I had changed in 4 years, so had UNHCR. When I first joined in 1975 there were some 500 people in the organisation, with an annual operating budget of around US$80m. This had swollen to around 800 staff members and a budget of some US$500m by the time I got back. The organisation continued to expand. By 2012, it had a budget of US$3.6 Billion and 7,685 staff posted in Geneva and around the world in 135 countries (including in 279 "remote" field offices). By 2022 the staff count had increased to over 17,000. What had started out as an attempt to solve the temporary problem of post WW2 displaced persons in Europe, became an all-embracing entity that spans the globe.[18]

In 1981, UNHCR was awarded the Nobel Prize for Peace, the citation mentioning, in particular, refugees from Vietnam, Afghanistan, and Ethiopia. (This was the second time it had received the award, the first occasion being in 1954 in recognition of its innovative approach to handling displaced people). It was also recognition for UNHCR doing its best to deal with the effects of problems largely created by other people. Refugees do not exist unless and until they flee their homes. The reasons for their flight may vary, but (leaving natural calamities aside) they are usually the result of political conflict, which the UN, throughout its existence, has tried to prevent or manage, obviously with varying degrees of success. And invariably, it is left to deal with the consequences of conflict.

And therefore the staff of the numerous UN agencies (particularly the more operational ones) are under permanent pressure to deal with problems that they did not create, cannot control, and for which ultimate solutions (if indeed these ever really exist) are usually beyond their capabilities and means. So it becomes an endless game of providing short term measures to relieve what everybody hopes is temporary suffering, but which often can become long-term dependency. However, long-term careers can be, and are, made on the

18. In 1950, the United Nations, the new global institution created in the aftermath of WW2, set up the office of the UN High Commissioner for Refugees (UNHCR), with a three-year mandate to complete the resettlement of the identified refugees in Europe, after which it was to be disbanded. Initially it had only 34 staff members and a first-year budget of $300,000. It became apparent that the refugee problem was not temporary, and successive three and five-year mandates followed until the General Assembly decided in 2003 to remove the time limitation and granted a permanent mandate until, in its own words, "the refugee problem is solved".

back of such human tragedies, albeit at the price of increasing cynicism and career-boosting opportunism.

I had already had an inkling of this in Thailand. Each boatload that arrived had to be dealt with, sheltered in the camps, interviewed, provided for, and eventually resettled as a permanent solution. But every boatload that was successfully put through the process was replaced with another, then another, and another, and this "pull" factor guaranteed a steady flow of new arrivals prepared to risk the crossing.

I was increasingly disquieted by the prospect of the endless treadmill of humanitarian work – seemingly doomed, like Sisyphus, to roll the boulder of temporary relief up one mountain of suffering only to see it roll back down the other side to yet another. Because of UNHCR's officially temporary status, permanent contracts for staff did not exist. The next best thing was an "indefinite" contract, which was the holy grail for all staff members, especially those from what was then still called the developing world. I had been awarded such a contract when I arrived back in Geneva but hadn't got around to signing it.

Finally, the head of the Personnel Division, a charming man, (who at the time was Kofi Annan, subsequently the Secretary General of the UN) called me in and asked why I hadn't signed. I tried to explain some of what I was feeling and that I didn't want to get locked into that way of life at such an early stage in my career. He kindly told me to get a grip and just sign the contract, lest there were a risk of it being withdrawn. He suggested that if it turned out that I wasn't happy, I could always leave later. He was right of course.

With the contract securing a future in UNHCR in my pocket, the restiveness did not abate; if anything it intensified, despite or probably due to the work. This was both interesting and challenging, albeit in a different way than I had been used to, being much more process-driven, bureaucratic, constraining, and requiring an endless search for consensus. I was in charge of the fast-growing Cambodian relief programme, which eventually had a budget of $100m.

When the crisis of the influx of Khmer Rouge followers first hit and UNHCR was asked to respond, in October 1979 a small team under Zia Rizvi was assembled (and labelled "high level" for the benefit of the Thai Government and donors). I was selected to be on it since I was the only person in the Headquarters with recent first-hand experience of the situation on the ground.

So not long after returning to Geneva, I was back on a flight to Bangkok (this time uneventful) with the team to assess the situation on the ground. Our first appointment was to have tea at Government House with the Prime Minister, General Kriangsak Chomanand. As I knew my way around

the border area, I was dispatched there to try and get up to date information about refugee movements and conditions, meeting up with the rest of the team at the site of a large new camp about to be built at Khao I Dang near Aranyaprathet. It would eventually at one time, briefly, become the largest concentration of Khmers in the world, housing some 150,000 people, but at the time it was just a muddy field, with the first busloads of shattered people scattered around, too weak to help themselves.

They had been living on the Cambodian side of the border for some months, under the control of the Khmer Rouge who had forced them to accompany them when the regime was driven out of Phnom Penh by the Vietnamese. They had had no access to food or medical care, and many had died within reach of the Thai border but forbidden to cross it by their leaders and the uncompromising attitude of the Thai Army.

This was finally relaxed, and UNHCR and the other agencies were expected to take care of them. My brief trip along the border had not resulted in any concrete details – just confirmation that there were many thousands of people in desperate need of help on the other side, under the control of various different political factions, but nobody knew exactly how many.

Our mission came to the conclusion that an assistance programme of US$100m would be required, and UNHCR was ultimately named as the lead agency to oversee it, much to the chagrin of the other agencies such as the ICRC and UNICEF who endlessly squabbled over the bragging rights of being responsible for delivering food assistance to and across the border. [19]

After a week in Thailand, more meetings with the Government and with the Ambassadors of the main donor countries, the team returned to Geneva to prepare for the activation of the new programme for which I was to be the Desk Officer. I settled quickly into the life of an international bureaucrat in the Centre William Rappard, half of which had by then been taken over by UNHCR. I shared a spacious two-man office overlooking the park with Larry Emler, a soft-spoken young American and we were assigned a highly competent, if occasionally temperamental, Iranian secretary, Zohreh Mobasser.

It was a fine existence, and the flavour of the team was greatly improved with the arrival of Pierre Jambor from Bangkok in early 1980, posted back to HQ to run the in-Cambodia assistance programme. When I first arrived, the head of the Asia Regional Bureau was a genial Dutchman of the old school, Fritz Hordijker, who had a convivial habit of occasionally inviting his staff for lunch in small Vaudois village restaurants to search out regional specialities, bits of which he would routinely decorate his tie with. Sadly, he retired at the end of 1979, to be replaced by Sampatkumar, a

---

19. It was a squalid, complicated and riveting story that was very well dissected by William Shawcross in his book "The Quality of Mercy".

wily and highly political Indian with whom one always had to be on one's guard, and whose very blonde Norwegian wife I remember spoke English with an Indian accent. My immediate superior was Rob van Leewen, a complex American of Dutch extraction who had spent some years in Indonesia, and who was also highly political. So between the two of them the atmosphere in the office was usually highly charged.

Social life was good, varied, even if relatively unexciting. I took up regular squash again, and even managed, selectively, to give a few lessons (generally to enthusiastic young women). There was an active squash club with a membership mainly drawn from the numerous UN agencies, and it was of sufficiently high quality to host an (amateur) Open Tournament which attracted some good overseas players. An even more serious competition was the Monte Carlo (Amateur) Open, to which a small team of club members travelled down to compete in. None of us advanced very far, but I since I knew the rules of the game, I was asked to umpire some of the matches, including the final (which I think was won by a Rhodesian tennis player).

But with the coming of the Spring, my restlessness resurfaced stronger than ever, and it was at the suggestion of a friend that I began to think about taking an MBA. I therefore applied to both IMD (later to become IMEDE) in Lausanne and to INSEAD in Fontainebleau and was interviewed by both institutions. IMD's intake in those days was only around 60 a year, while INSEAD's was 240. Both offered me a place; IMD's academic year started in January, INSEAD's in September. I was keen to get started and when INSEAD's offer arrived, only two weeks before the semester was due to begin, I accepted it immediately.

I quickly applied for study leave, which was granted, drove over to Fontainebleau one weekend to find a place to stay, and was extremely lucky to find a room with private bathroom in a beautiful, converted 14th century water mill outside Episy-sur-Loing, located to the south of the Fontainebleau forest. I returned to Geneva, managed to sell my bed and bookcase, handed over the work to my replacement, tidied my desk, said my farewells, packed my meagre belongings into the car, and headed north. I had just turned 29, and although I had once more loved living in Geneva, I was excited to be on the move again.

Business school was extremely hard work, very satisfying, and proved to be an immensely rewarding interlude. I had heard that companies came on campus each year to interview candidates, and naively expected to be offered a job, but as I hadn't really thought about what I wanted to do and 1981 was a time of deep recession, there was almost no interest in a freshly minted MBA with a background of working in refugee camps. I did manage to obtain a few interviews, one with a bank that no longer exists (First Chicago, which was subsumed into Banc One in 1998, and ultimately became part of Chase) but that came to naught when I was asked what I had done in the UN. I enthusiastically launched into a lengthy description before realising that I was getting zero feedback. I stopped talking. Silence. It was clear that I had blown my chances when the only question I was asked was whether I had written a book about my experiences. Very evidently, there was no "fit" with the company culture. The only company that was interested in my background was L'Oreal, but at the time I hadn't ever envisaged the possibility of working for a female cosmetics company, and rashly turned down the opportunity to take it further. It was the only one I was offered.

At the end of the year, I had arranged to visit Thailand and Burma with a couple of friends, and by the time I got back home the office was asking when I would return. A six-month

posting in Manila had opened up to help handle the resettlement of the Vietnamese boat people (my speciality),
and since my need to earn money was again acute, I accepted
the position, went back to Geneva for a few days, and shortly
afterwards flew out to the Philippines.

20

Manila

I t was good to be back in Asia, and very good to be earning again. The UNHCR office was located in the Makati business district, and for the first few weeks I stayed at a variety of hotels before finding a small apartment in a building on Roxas Boulevard opposite Manila Bay and its spectacular sunsets. It was not the first time I had been to Manila, since on my departure from Thailand in 1979, I had stayed with my good friend Hank Hendrickson who, after Thailand, had been back in the USA to train in the Tagalog language before being posted to the US Embassy in Manila as political counsellor. He was still there when I got back, and through him I luckily inherited a lively American-dominated social scene.

The Philippines is an interesting mix of cultures and bloodlines. Ruled by Spain for 333 years, it was then under the "tutelage" of the USA for a further 47. Geographically, it is widely dispersed over 7,000 islands, in which over 180 different ethnic groups have been identified. UNHCR's role there was limited, and certainly less active than in Thailand or Malaysia.

In 1980, the Philippines Government had agreed to host a refugee processing centre on the Bataan peninsula some 3 hours north of Manila, for which the UNHCR provide the funds for its construction. (Bataan gained notoriety for the WW2 "Death March" after the surrender of US and Filipino forces in 1942).

The centre was established to alleviate some of the pressure in the holding centres of the neighbouring countries of first asylum to which boats from Vietnam continued to aim for. Once approved for resettlement, refugees in these camps who could be moved to the Philippines where, under the auspices of voluntary agencies such as the International Catholic Migration Commission and World Relief, they were able to learn English, attend cultural and work orientation classes, be screened and treated for any diseases (mainly tuberculosis), and where the children could attend school. Most were destined for the USA, but some went to Australia, Canada, or Europe.

The head of the UN office in Manila was my former boss from Geneva, Sampatkumar, but as there appeared to be few issues that he thought required his personal attention, he spent quite a lot of time outside the office. His deputy was an Englishman on secondment from the Foreign Office, who was unused to, and certainly had a low point of tolerance for, the frustrations of working in Asia. From time to time a boat would arrive directly in the Philippines, and the occupants would have to be interviewed and registered. Aside from the Bataan centre, a smaller camp had been established on the outskirts of Puerto Princesa the provincial capital of Palawan, the long finger of an island which lay to the southwest of Manila pointing towards Borneo. The camp was also well served by the voluntary agencies in terms of educational and health needs, and while most of the occupants had already been approved for resettlement, any new direct arrivals were interviewed in the camp to await their turn.

Duties with UNHCR were therefore relatively light, leaving plenty of time for social activities, including regular tennis, and golf at the weekends on one of the many fine courses in and close to Manila. Since the Americans were everybody's best friend, our golf outings would often include one or more colourful Filipino political figures or fixers. A friend from INSEAD had given me an introduction to Harry Wilken, a fine Scotsman from Elgin who was based in Manila with Jardine Matheson, and through him I met his colleagues in the firm and others in the British business community, which provided a nice balance to social life. Harry became a firm friend, who I subsequently met up with quite often after he moved to Hong Kong. He lived life to the full and was later stationed in Bermuda as President of Jardine Matheson International. Sadly, he died in 2010 while still in the post.

The Philippine islands are situated on one of the most un-stable parts of the earth's crust, the western edge of the Pacific ring of fire where the Philippine tectonic plate slides under the Eurasian plate, and in the short time I was posted in Manila there were 3 minor quakes. The first was in working hours when the whole office started rattling, papers and equipment fell on the floor, and we all had to evacuate the building and stand in the middle of the street for a while, before we were allowed back in. The second was stronger; I happened to be lying on my bed on a Sunday afternoon, and the whole apartment started to sway. I had read that in such an event one of the places to head for was the door frame, which I duly did, but that was swaying and creaking alarmingly as well. There were two distinct strong tremors, but then it all calmed down again. The third time was much less noticeable, but by that time I had become relatively blasé about them. In my very limited experience, the fact that what we imagine to be *terra firma* turns out not to be as solid as we thought was very disturbing, and I have no desire to live through one again.

The other natural phenomena that are features of the Philippines are volcano eruptions and typhoons, and while I was spared the former, I was witness to an impressive and powerful typhoon that tore through the central part of Luzon, the main island, and Manila. The local staff told me it was only medium scale, since the typhoon season strikes every year, sometimes with catastrophic results.

As the end of the year approached, it emerged that both Sampatkumar and his deputy had decided to take leave over the Christmas and New Year period, so by default I became, temporarily, the most senior person in the office. An invitation arrived at the office for the New Year's Eve party that the President hosted each year at his official residence, Malacanang Palace, for the diplomatic Corps and representatives of the UN agencies. It was addressed to the Head of the UNHCR Mission. I felt obliged to accept.

I had remembered to bring my dinner jacket (which in fact I had already worn for a St. Andrews Ball organised by Harry Wilken at the Manila Polo Club, which turned out to have a sprung dance floor, perfect for reeling). Formally attired, I was driven in the office car to the Palace (first built by the Spaniards in 1750, it served as the official seat of power for the colonial rulers), then let the driver go as he was keen to celebrate new year with his family. I was by far the youngest guest at the party (apart from the president's children), and on arrival joined the queue to meet the hosts, Ferdinand Marcos and his glamorous and bejewelled wife, Imelda. I had been put on a table seated next to the elegant and cultured wife of the Egyptian Ambassador, with whom I subsequently took a couple of turns on the dance floor. At one stage we found ourselves dancing next to Imelda, who was doing her supple best to get her dancing partner to loosen up. This was the Chinese Ambassador, looking distinctly uncomfortable, stiff in his starched Mao suit buttoned up to the neck, and barely moving, as if his limbs were made of wood. He just looked ridiculous in the tropical heat and colour. But the novelty of the evening eventually began to flag, and as soon as New Year struck, I slipped out and drove through the deserted streets to Hank's house, where I knew a more relaxed party was going on.

A week later, I again had the chance to don my dinner jacket and attend a dinner for the diplomatic corps and heads of agencies, on this occasion invited by the legendary Carlos P. Romero, the Foreign Minister, (I think to celebrate his birthday). In his long and distinguished career, he had been a journalist, diplomat, had served 8 Filipino presidents, had been an aide to General Douglas Macarthur during the war, narrowly missed out on becoming Secretary-General of the United Nations but was President of UN Security Council four times, and had written 22 books.

I joined the queue of guests to meet the host and his American wife, and when my turn came, he fixed me with a gimlet eye and asked what my role was (it felt more like "what are you doing here?"). I explained the absence of the more senior staff, expressed appreciation of my good fortune to be able to attend and pay respects on behalf of the UNHCR, whereupon he smiled and said he hoped that I would have a good time. A mightily impressive man, all 4 foot 8 inches of him, and unquestionably one of the great Asian figures of the 20th century.

I came across the Marcos' again a few weeks later, when they decided to pay a visit to the Bataan centre. By this time Sampatkumar and his deputy had returned from their holidays, and so I played a supporting role in the UNHCR delegation that was obliged to attend. A dais had been erected for the visit, from which Marcos was to address the assembled crowd.

I had a seat in the second row, just behind the President and his wife. Seated to my right happened to be George

Hamilton, the perma-tanned minor Hollywood film star to whom Imelda had taken a fancy. He was friendly, didn't seem sure why he was there, and so I was able to explain a bit about the centre's origin and purpose. It was well known that by that time Marcos was on dialysis, and he had the puffiness of face that can reveal kidney disease. (He was also rumoured to be taking multiple local herbal concoctions to maintain his manly vigour). When he got up to give his short speech, he was clearly ailing; mumbling, and losing his place. Imelda was very on the ball, giving a discreet masterclass in both anticipating and prompting him on what he was to say, and it looked to me that even at that stage, she was the power behind the throne.

As my allotted time in Manila drew to a close, I began a dialogue with Headquarters about where I might go next. The only post on offer was as Field Officer in Somalia – or more precisely, in a location somewhere near the border with the disputed Ogaden region of Ethiopia, the origin of the displaced people being who were being helped. This did not appeal. A lot of pressure was applied, including flattering personal calls: "We need someone who can hit the ground running"; and "You're one of the few with relevant field experience" etc. There was no doubt a degree of truth in this but having invested time and money in an MBA degree, it was not something I was prepared to dissipate in the deserts of the north-eastern corner of Africa, no matter how desperate the need.

As no other options were offered, I therefore resigned, with a great – if temporary – sense of relief. It was a bit of a wrench to have to leave Manila and the friends I had made, but I knew that while the time there had been interesting, and great fun, it did not hold out any prospects for the future. I had been able to save up some money again, and had to think seriously about what I was going to do in the longer term.

Nobody in UNHCR reached out to encourage me to stay or provide a rationale as to why I should, and I had already worked out that given my background and personality, it was unlikely to be the best environment for me to flourish. I had been lucky; most of the time with UNHCR I had enjoyed huge autonomy and freedom of action, but that was unlikely to continue unless I were prepared to accept postings to remote field locations such as Somalia.

As soon as I got back home in March 1982, I started to look for jobs, and soon compiled a thick file of application letters and rejections, reflecting the sobering fact that in a UK recovering from the 1981 recession, the combination of an MBA degree (still relatively rare in those days) and working in refugee camps did not fit the recruitment criteria of the companies I applied to. I moved down to London to be closer to possible interviews, took up evening Japanese classes, and survived by making modest amounts of money from a recovering stock market, and even from a sugar trading deal.

Amongst other ideas, I initiated an attempt to become one of UNHCR's approved procurement suppliers and in late August 1983 flew over to Geneva to explore the possibility. Each year the agency bought increasing volumes of basic goods for its various programmes around the world, such as vehicles, blankets, tents, foodstuffs and clothing.[20] The head of procurement, an old friend from earlier days, explained in detail what I would need to do to become eligible for consideration in any bidding process. It sounded encouraging, and certainly something worth pursuing. I was planning to return to Asia to be able to source goods from the region, and before leaving the office dropped in to see another old friend Denis McNamara. In parting I told him of my plan to go back to Asia and said that if there were any short-term consultancy opportunities available, I might be interested.

Unexpectedly, a week later, Denis called me. There was a problem in Bangkok with a programme that had been set up to tackle the piracy attacks on the Vietnamese boats, and they needed someone to sort it out. Would I be interested? 10 days later I flew out to Geneva and on to Bangkok.

---

20. Procurement of goods and services is nowadays huge business in UNHCR, handled by a Division of Emergency, Security and Supply, and a global Supply Management and Logistics Service. In hindsight, it was evidently a good growth sector to target.

21

Regional Anti-Piracy Co-ordinator

T he purpose of this visit to Bangkok was for me to carry out an assessment of the situation, and report back to Geneva. The publicity generated by Ted Schweitzer's activities (described earlier) had resulted in the marine detachment being posted to Koh Kra, and the build-up of considerable public pressure on Thailand to take action against its fishing boats. The US had provided some funds to the Thai Navy on a bilateral basis to refurbish a couple of patrol boats, and there was a consensus (at least in Western embassies and at the UN) that "something had to be done". It was made clear to me by the Protection Officer of the UNHCR office in Bangkok (a young American lawyer) that he wasn't that interested in the additional burden that the programme had given him, he was more than happy to hand over all anti-piracy matters to me, and was keen to introduce me to the Thai counterparts as his successor in all things to do with piracy.

The Bangkok office's suggestions as to what could be done included arranging both international and regional conferences on piracy, improving the collection of statistics of attacks, victims and arrests, and creating clear lines of authority and responsibility between Bangkok and Geneva to avoid overlap. In short, typically bureaucratic ideas. What was immediately clear was that I would be able to, and indeed would have to, define my own role, and that appealed greatly.

I would be based in Bangkok, report to Geneva, but would have to keep the regional office informed.

The next step was to meet someone from the US Embassy, who confirmed that the US had so far committed limited funds to the anti-piracy efforts that it wouldn't withdraw, but that any further funding would be conditional on the Thais showing goodwill. The Thai Government had submitted an equipment shopping list of $36m, which had been whittled down to $3.6m, but this amount still had to be found. Twelve countries had apparently expressed interest in supporting anti-piracy efforts.

I then attended a meeting convened by the head of the National Security Committee (NSC), at which representatives of the Royal Thai Navy (RTN), the Police, the Marine Police, and the Harbour Department were all present. The NSC chief opened by suggesting that, in the spirit of the Orderly Departure Programme[21] that had been agreed in 1979, perhaps the UN could eliminate the problems by sending ships to pick up the refugees as they left Vietnam? A neat solution for Thailand perhaps, but hardly practical. He said that he had discussed with his colleagues in the other agencies and that the idea of a co-ordination centre might work, but only if appropriately funded. He also opined that the Customs Department could or should have a role as, aside from its key role in raising revenue for the government, it might be able to provide some useful information. Fortunately, this idea was immediately rejected by the other agencies, while the RTN insisted that its warships were already assigned an anti-piracy role and that co-ordination already existed between the different agencies.

---

21. The UN estimated that from 1980 until 1997 over 620,000 Vietnamese were resettled abroad under the Orderly Departure Programme, of whom some 460,000 (74%) went to the United States.

As the meeting progressed, I was able to make a few early observations: (i) there was little or no co-ordination between the agencies because their responsibilities were all different; (ii) the RTN considered itself above all the others since it was involved in defence of the nation, not crime-fighting; (iii) the Harbour Department was clearly not used to being included in such a group and was struggling to modernise, claiming not even to have computerised records; (iv) the Police were reluctant participants since it meant they would have to be more active in trying to identify and apprehend Thai citizens for attacks on the disliked Vietnamese; and (v) the only thing that attracted universal support was the idea of obtaining funds for their slice of any programme that might be agreed. Armed with this information, I returned to Geneva to report back.

After discussions with the Director of International Protection, Michel Moussalli, a tall and urbane Lebanese to whom I was to report in the first instance (and who was therefore my direct boss), I agreed to take on the seemingly thankless task of trying to retrieve the UNHCR's effort to make sense of its anti-piracy activities. For this I was given the fine title of "Regional Anti-Piracy Co-ordinator". Since the attacks on the refugees had attracted so much media attention, piracy had become a popular cause for other UN agencies. The International Maritime Organisation thought it should be involved since it was the UN agency most active in maritime safety (UNHCR agreed to pass on information on current activities). UNCTAD (the trade organisation), said it was preparing a report on worldwide piracy and invited UNHCR to submit ideas relating to its impact on refugees. (The UNHCR programme was the only one in the world at the time with a specific anti-piracy target). I was happy to leave liaison with these other UN agencies to colleagues in Geneva.

I went back home for a couple of weeks while Geneva took care of the administrative details for issuing my contract, obtaining a visa, and making travel arrangements. I returned on October 3rd for a final briefing and to begin initial co-ordination duties – with the Desk Officers; for Malaysia, for Thailand, for Vietnam, and for Singapore, Indonesia, and the Philippines; with the Protection Division; and with the Public Information Division. It was reported that the Thai Government had finally approved a programme of support worth US$2.71m, the bulk of it to be provided by the US Government. The Thai Co-ordinating HQ was supposed to be in Songkhla, where the official liaison between the RTN and the Police was to occur. So, it at least sounded as though things were beginning to come together.

But the fact of the matter was that there were many differences of opinion across the spectrum; in Thailand amongst the different entities; in the UN between the agencies; and within the UNHCR itself, between regional offices and inside headquarters. Some thought it a poorly conceived idea that could create more problems than it solved, while others wanted to be involved (because it was relatively high profile). One such was the UNHCR representative in Singapore, Shashi Tharoor,[22] who felt that since Singapore was one of the world's

---

22. A British-born Indian, Tharoor joined UNHCR in 1978 and was the representative in Singapore between 1981 and 1984. Highly intelligent, eloquent and articulate, his Wikipedia entry states that "during the boat people crisis he led the organisation's rescue efforts at sea and succeeding in resettling a backlog of Vietnamese refugees." In fact, there were almost no Vietnamese refugees in Singapore, and no rescues at sea were launched from there. In 1989 he was appointed special assistant to the Under-Secretary-General (USG) for Special Political Affairs (SPA), who in 1993 became Kofi Annan. (It is worth remembering that the Rwandan genocide occurred in 1994, which the SPA, the relevant UN agency, did nothing to prevent despite the desperate urging

epicentres for maritime piracy, his office should be consulted. He was alone in this opinion.

It was clear that, like every UN project, its survival would depend on whether sufficient funds could be raised from donors. At the time, the US Government was alone in backing it as part of a separate programme of military assistance to the Thai Government, although both the German and Norwegian governments were offering bilateral assistance in kind (mainly in the form of training). The creation of the UNHCR programme meant that all such bilateral efforts could be focussed into one project, but whether it could be made more effective was to be my responsibility. Moussalli wanted to report back to the donors before the end of the year, so the first priority was to gather reliable information to present to a donors meeting; what the funds were being spent on; what future donations would be invested in; what input the Thai Government would provide; the degree to which mooted proposals were in fact acceptable to it; ways in which the Thai programme could be strengthened; how much funding the US might be able to contribute. While there was a lot of goodwill, it was likely to be temporary, and would have to be backed up by concrete actions.

---

of the head of the UN Assistance Mission in the country at the time, Canadian General Romeo Dallaire, whom I met at the Edinburgh Book Festival some years later). In 1996, Tharoor became the UN's Director of Communications and Special Projects, then Executive Assistant to Annan when the latter became Secretary-General in 1997. In 2002, he continued his rise, becoming USG for Communications and Public Information. He stood for election as UN Secretary General when Annan retired in 2005 but among other things was regarded as being too close to his former boss and came second to Ban Ki-Moon. After his UN career, he went on to become a politician in India and a prolific author, dogged by controversy in both his personal and private lives.

22

Getting started

Since the programme affected all the littoral countries of the South China Sea, their inter-relationships were important. Historically, the area was a rich source of fish, but increasingly intense competition between the fishing fleets of the various countries, reflecting their growing wealth and increasing demand, meant that fish stocks were declining fast due to over-fishing. Thai boats would travel to fish off the coasts of Vietnam, Malaysia, and Indonesia, and were notorious for their piratical tendencies.

The Malaysians were keen to stop Thai boats attacking Malay boats – Thai boats on contract to Singaporean traders had been reported as plundering whatever vessels they came across on their route home – Vietnamese or Malaysian. The Malaysians were therefore keen to support a programme that would curtail piracy, but since it was to be carried out by Thai agencies, there was some scepticism that it could be effective. But at the same time there was little appetite for the Malaysian navy to take action against Thai boats that were attacking Vietnamese.

The boat people were another source of friction between the Thais and the Malaysians – both countries tried to push off new arrivals to the other, with the Thais usually being the more successful, in part because there were larger facilities in Malaysia to handle the refugees, and there were far fewer reports of attacks by Malaysian fishing boats. But the governments of both countries shared the suspicion that the Vietnamese government was deliberately allowing the boats to leave in order to increase tension between them.

When I arrived back in Thailand in late 1983, the situation was fluid and uneasy, and while the Thai agencies were seemingly adjusting to their additional new responsibilities, it was more in form than substance. I therefore set about arranging to meet all the key people in the different agencies to ascertain what they thought they were supposed to be doing, the extent to which they were doing it, and whether they had better ideas to improve the programme.

The South China Sea, and the Straits of Malacca in particular, have a long tradition of piracy. Early accounts exist of attacks on ships plying the India-China trading route over a thousand years ago, and there are colourful and sanguinary tales over many centuries of pirate activity from Japan, Vietnam, China, and the Malay states. In part this has been a result of local economic hardship, ungovernable stretches of coastline, an absence of central authority, and opportunism. But a large part is explained by international trade flows and geography.

An estimated 30% of global sea traffic passes through the Straits of Malacca each year, which has long been a focal point for piracy because of its narrow width, which forces ships to slow down. Still today, piracy is an occasional problem in the area.

Another issue was the nature of the Thai fishing industry. Men became fishermen either because that was a family tradition in the coastal villages they came from, or they moved from other provinces, often escaping from the consequences of criminal activity there. Conditions on board the boats were primitive and dangerous; pay was low and dependent on the volume and value of the weekly catch, which with growing competition was under increasing pressure. Resistance to the

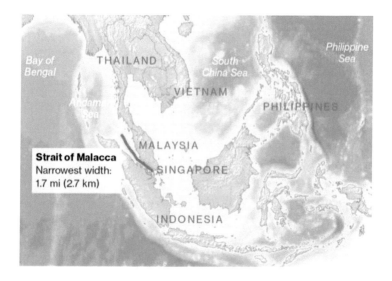

temptation of committing piracy against defenceless Vietnam-ese was therefore understandably weak.

Of course, the Thais agencies knew all this far better than we did, and the head of the NSC had been overheard to say that at least US$30m would be needed for an effective anti-piracy programme. There was never any suggestion that the Thai Government itself would invest such an amount, since it really did not see the issue as a priority. International donors were very unlikely to provide so much money, and in any case wanted to see reports on how their donations to date had been invested. A third issue was that the Thai agencies were extremely reluctant to provide any reports on their activities, but since any future funding would be dependent on the donors receiving adequate information, improving such reporting was going to be one of my major tasks.

By this stage there had in fact already been some progress in Thailand's efforts to combat piracy. Some fishermen had been arrested in the wake of the assaults at Koh Kra described earlier, and their trial had begun in Bangkok. Naval patrol boats were reported to leave Songkhla port from time to time, even if what they did out of sight of land was not known. It was reported that Malaysia and Thailand had started to coordinate naval patrols along their joint maritime frontier, and the Chairman of the NSC had written a formal letter to the agencies involved requesting details of their 'implementation needs'. (This clearly necessitated my follow-up to help determine what those needs were and to keep them within practical bounds).

The Norwegian Government was about to invite officials from the Harbour Department to train in Norway on computerising the registration of fishing vessels. And the US Government was pushing the RTN for the deployment of (and by implication, offering the funding for) a larger patrol vessel. All this was a step change from even a few months earlier, and by 2004, Singapore, Malaysia, and Indonesia were to begin coordinated naval patrols in the Malacca Strait.

I continued my rounds of the donor country embassies. The second secretary of the British Embassy stated that HMG had no great interest in piracy as a problem per se, although since it was part of the refugee problem, there was concern at a personal level. HMG was not prepared to contribute any more funds to the project on the basis of the scanty existing reports, although it might reconsider at a later stage. The Defence Attaché was sceptical about the programmes' operational efficacy, but had not yet been to Songkhla, which he was due to visit the following month.

The Canadians and Australians, although both insistent that better information be provided, were largely supportive of the programme, in part because they had been and were still actively involved in the resettlement of the Vietnamese which meant that for them there was a degree of domestic awareness about the issue. The latter also had an ongoing commercial interest because the Royal Thai Navy was being given a new Hawker Pacific Nomad patrol plane as part of the programme. The other donor embassies (German, Switzerland, Netherlands, Norway, Italy, Denmark) were more modest contributors, content to show solidarity with the joint efforts which everybody recognised were being pushed (and largely funded) by the Americans.

Before heading down to Songkhla to visit the co-ordination centre, I had lunch with the representatives of Hawker Pacific (*"HP"*), who were negotiating directly with the RTN for the supply of the Nomad patrol plane. The RTN was insisting on a Thai-language contract, the final version of which had yet to be agreed, but HP had already set in motion the order for the aircraft plus avionics, pending the signing of the official contract.

Return to my earlier stamping ground brought back a load of memories, and I was greeted at the hotel as a long-lost friend. I paid a courtesy call on the Governor's office before attending a meeting at the RTN base where I was met by Admiral Vichit and 3 naval captains. As expected, the RTN was taking its participation in the programme seriously, and as the most senior of the agencies involved, it wanted to set an example.

It had four main items on its agenda – 1) the installation of landing lights at the Songkhla airstrip that was included in the budget for the forthcoming year; 2) the acquisition of the new Nomad aircraft; 3) the (much improved) situation on Koh Kra where a marine detachment had been stationed; and 4) the question of paying for information. The last issue was the only really sensitive topic, and clearly something that the RTN felt was beneath them, but since it was clear there was a need for it, after discussion it was agreed that such payments could be covered by the "Information Gathering" item in the budget.

The next meeting was with the local Marine Police, who were keen to find out when the new fast patrol craft that had been included in the current year's budget would be delivered. They said that there was daily radio contact with the RTN, and that they dispatched regular sea patrols, so we discussed the benefits of these being timed on an irregular basis. The Marine Police had also chartered a couple of fishing trawlers that they sent out to observe the fishing fleet, but it was assumed that everybody knew which boats were playing this role. Two new hydrojet patrol boats were expected to be delivered soon, one to be based at Surat Thani to the north, the other at Songkhla. Since this was a coastline of some 400 miles, they thought that more boats would be a good idea as it would enable more comprehensive coverage of the area.

I then went over to meet the 4th Region Police Commander to introduce myself and talk about the programme. In terms of budgetary support, the Police had benefitted the least from it up until then, and the discussion quickly turned to how this might be remedied. While the RTN and Marine Police were largely involved in prevention rather than detention, there was no question that the harder part of the project (gathering information, making arrests, filing charges etc.) was the responsibility of the Police, and I could see that without its co-operation, concrete results would be hard to achieve. I suggested that they might like to come up with a list of items that would be helpful.

The final visit of this introductory trip was back to the US Consulate, where, as before, the (new) Consul was helpful and informative. He mentioned that the US Drug Enforcement Agency (DEA) had introduced a reward system for information leading to the seizure of drugs or detention of dealers and wondered whether a similar system could be put in place to help track and rescue abductees from the boats. We talked about the potential benefits and drawbacks to this idea, and while it was clear that such a system would certainly be open to abuse, and even likely to be seen as an incentive to fishing crews to abduct more Vietnamese girls, the idea, carefully targeted, was nonetheless worth exploring.

Further meetings over the next few days brought up new ideas. The Police thought that it might be useful to hold public meetings in coastal villages to explain the programme and to offer rewards for information. The Harbour Department was planning to introduce a new registration system for fishing boats along the coats, using a numerical code to identify the province of origin and individual boat (e.g., 01-1000 for Narathiwat, 02-1000 for Pattani, etc.) and suppressing any creative "fancy lettering and numbers". Fishing boat owners tended to move their operating base from time to time and increasing numbers of boats had been coming from ports to the north (largely due to overfishing in the upper Gulf of Siam). It had also been suggested that boats would have to have their registration number painted on the stern as well as on each side of the bow (the standard practice, which made identification of any boat fleeing the scene of an attack practically impossible).

At each successive meeting, it appeared that the different agencies had begun to realise that the programme, which hitherto had been seen as an intrusion imposed on them by the National Security Council under pressure from foreigners, could in fact be of benefit to them in carrying out their regular duties, and I tried to emphasise this aspect of it. Part of the burden they had to bear was the reporting for donors, the co-ordination responsibility for which had been handed over to Chulalongkorn University, which had to clear each report with the NSC before release. Yet another link in the chain, it gave each agency the ability to palm off any direct query – "we have submitted our report to the University"; "the report has been sent for translation" etc.

The agency that had most immediately grasped the implications of the modest anti-piracy programme was the RTN, which had long experience of dealing with direct foreign military assistance programmes (in particular) the USA. The USA, in turn, had run and managed such programmes for many years, and were expert in monitoring and reporting on them. Since the anti-piracy investment was being taken from a budget that apparently included other direct bilateral support, there was always an element of doubt as to how much would actually be delivered through the UNHCR, and there was a certain amount of tension about the extent and quality of the reporting that was required. In the eyes of the USA, maximum control of expenditures would be exercised through JUSMAG[23] (the Joint US Military Advisory Group); minimum control through the UNHCR. It was another reminder that foreign funding for the programme was and would be heavily contingent on adequate reporting.

The official structure of the programme was an agreement between the Thai National Security Council and UNHCR. The individual agencies prepared their own proposals and budgets and sent these to the NSC for review and amendment before presentation to UNHCR. Geneva's attitude (understandably) was that it preferred to negotiate the budget with the NSC, and not with the individual agencies. This meant that my co-ordinating role had to be done at different levels, the most obvious being between the UNHCR offices in Geneva and Bangkok, and between UNHCR Bangkok and the NSC. In fact,

23. JUSMAGTHAI is the U.S. Security Cooperation Office in Thailand. Its chief is part of the US Pacific Command in Hawaii but is also directly responsible to the U.S. Ambassador to Thailand.

the more useful aspect turned out to be the co-ordination both with the Thai agencies and even between them, below the level of the NSC contacts. For that I had to ensure that each agency saw me as being on its side in helping them draw up and defend their budgets to the NSC.

Co-ordination with each agency often meant that such activities also had to include co-ordination within each agency, since anti-piracy activities were new and could cut across traditional lines of command. Therefore, information and knowledge sometimes had to be gathered or shared between departments that did not normally communicate. The assistance budgets were sometimes a source of envy between departments – why one should receive material assistance, while another should not.

No agency had just a single person with whom I could be in contact, since in each one the level of seniority and responsibility of the people I had to deal with were all different. For example, while I had direct contact with the Deputy Director-General of the Harbour Department, I also had to work with the Director of the Registration and Licence Division that was handling the new computer registration system donated by the Norwegian Government.

Unlike the Thai agencies, each donor government at least had a single point of contact for what was, for most of them, a minor issue. I got to know the various responsible officers quite well as l made the rounds of the embassies to report on progress and get their feedback, which usually consisted of complaints about the inadequate reporting.

Already pressure was building for a new donor's meeting to be held in Geneva before the end of the year (1983), even though by this time it was already the end of October. This initiative was being pushed mainly by the US government, which had allocated a sum that it wanted to commit as soon as possible towards a renewed programme, for fear that Congress might withdraw it. The condition was that it should not be a bilateral (government to government) donation, and that the new budget when presented by UNHCR should be larger than just the US contribution so that other countries could be seen to be helping as well. At the same time, another tranche of funds from the existing year's programme was about to be handed over to the NSC.

In early November I was asked to accompany a delegation of embassy officials from the USA, the UK, and Germany on a fact-finding mission to Songkhla. We were given plausible briefings at the RTN Command Centre, followed by a brief outing in an RTN patrol craft (within sight of land) and a flight in the Nomad aircraft. It was the RTN's show, and it did it well, but there was little evidence of the participation of any of the other agencies.

The British official observed that the existing naval pro-gramme might unfairly be judged to comprise nothing more than what the RTN might usually be expected to carry out, and it called into question why the international community should be funding such normal Thai naval duties. The German delegate thought that more information about abductees would have been useful. Overall, the visit seemed to go down well, no doubt in part because it provided a good excuse for the embassy staff to get out of Bangkok and visit the south.

Within UNHCR there was still some talk (and in some quar-ters, hope) that the Malaysian government might get involved in the programme, and the representative in Kuala Lumpur was asked to sound out the authorities there. I believed that it was highly unlikely, since it would be seen by the Thais as an anti-Thai measure, and the Malaysians were unlikely to want to provoke that kind of sentiment. UNHCR was trying to explore the possibility of introducing a reward system for any Malaysian fishermen who brought to land any abductees taken off Thai boats, and it was also considering the creation of a "plaque of appreciation" for anyone who might give material help to refugees or piracy victims. The German government had made an offer of a spotter plane to the Malaysian government, but since the latter was being "very slow" in reacting to the offer, it was not thought likely that it would accept. So while there was no shortage of goodwill gestures on the part of well-meaning foreigners, there was a reluctance on the part of the host country to accede to anything that might be seen as further encouragement to the Vietnamese.

My discussions with the various Thai agencies could be disarmingly frank, and sometimes contradictory to the official line coming out of the NSC. One on visit to the Police Department, while UNHCR had been led to believe that the NSC had already asked the agencies for their budgets, the officer said that he had not received any such formal request. He thought it would only take about 10 days to prepare, and that he was happy to review it with me before submission. He added that they reported every month to the NSC but could do much more if required to, or if they were asked to. All this underlined the importance of maintaining good relations with as many points of contact as possible in the relevant agencies, while at the same time exercising maximum discretion to avoid any loss of face either between the different levels of the agencies themselves or between them and the NSC.

But occasionally it was necessary to reveal some of the inconsistencies in either the facts or what was being reported. I had my own points of contact at the NSC, was able to develop an increasingly good relationship with them, and so could call on their help when there were genuine issues of miscommunication from or between the agencies, or of forgetfulness (which did occur quite frequently, mainly in the form of delayed requests for intelligence from the agencies, or the provision of information or the issuance of instructions to the agencies). It became a game of polite probing and giving gentle reminders to ensure that what was being said was, in fact, being done.

It also created useful informal channels of communication with the agencies, which quickly learned that there was a source of information out with their particular silo. An example was that one day I received a call from an officer in Naval Intelligence, who had heard that a new anti-piracy initiative had been launched (without official permission) by a private US group, and that its crew members had been informed that they were being funded by the ICRC (the International Committee of the Red Cross). I was able to check this story with the ICRC representative in Bangkok who denied any involvement, confirming the RTN's suspicions that it was in fact an independently-funded exercise. The multi-level approach got to the stage where the RTN asked if someone in its Operations Division could call me directly to discuss its draft budget, to which of course I agreed.

Meanwhile tensions between Thailand and Malaysia continued. I received a call from the UNHCR office in Kuala Lumpur reporting on a recent incident whereby Thai fishing boats had sought shelter in Malaysian waters from a storm, and 2 abducted Vietnamese women had taken advantage of being close to an island and jumped into the sea to escape. The Thai boats had then threatened to attack the island, resulting in the Malaysian police and Marines being called, 2 Thai fishing boats being impounded, and 12 Thais arrested. While it did nothing to improve relations between the two countries, it was a stark reminder that the rationale for the programme was still as valid as ever.

While the human costs were still being counted, the

programme nonetheless had to grind through the realities of dealing with Government agencies and their procurement regulations. Under the current year's budget, the Harbour Department had been given funds to buy a new computer system, and under its procurement rules, an official tender had to be issued to prospective suppliers. I was informed that 15 companies had shown interest, that the tender period was to close on 23rd December, and that it would take 1-2 more months to assess the bids for relevance and price before a winner could be selected and a contract awarded. Transformation to the digital age would take time.

In late November 1983, the British Embassy asked me to brief the head of the political section in the UK's Foreign and Commonwealth Office, who was passing through Bangkok, on the anti-piracy programme. Given that the UK was then engaged in the Falklands War, it was surprising that the programme received even this degree of attention, but it turned out that it had been the subject of a Granada TV documentary that had been broadcast in Britain a few days earlier. I never got a chance to see the film but was told that a UNHCR officer had said on camera that the attacks on Vietnamese boats had the tacit approval of the Thai Government because they made the Vietnamese think twice about making the crossing, and that the film producer had managed to find a Thai fisherman who had claimed to have earned around £50,000 from attacks on refugee boats.

The documentary had also questioned why the RTN's suppression unit should continue to receive funds from the UK Government and the international community, since it had never caught any pirates. The film had ended by asking why the piracy problem had been forgotten. Even if there were no longer so many lurid incidents to attract the attention of the UK media, the short answer was that it hadn't been forgotten, but my unflagging efforts to draw out budget details from the agencies and encourage some degree of performance that could be measured was far from headline material.

By this time, given that new budget details were slow to emerge from the NSC and that there was still some scepticism among the donors about the efficacy of the programme, Moussalli had wisely decided not to hold a new donors' meeting before the end of the year as originally hoped for. This took some of the immediate pressure off, and my rounds of the agencies continued.

The Marine Police were due to receive new patrol boats, one of which had been funded under the UN programme. I told them that for a report to the donors, photographic evidence of an operating patrol would be helpful, and suggested that a UN officer (by implication, me) should be allowed to go out on patrol with them. This they thought was forbidden under their operating rules, but instead they offered to take any of the donors out for a demonstration patrol. An event that I would also have to co-ordinate.

I didn't want to talk only to officers at the Bangkok Headquarters, so also visited some of the local bases located in the provinces. At the Laem Ngob base, near the Cambodian border, I was told that the base had only one 60-foot patrol boat (its other 100-foot boat having been reclaimed by Bangkok), and that there had been no anti-piracy patrols out of Bangkok for over a year due to other operational pressures. The officer I spoke to had indeed heard of UNHCR, mainly the fact that it had helped the RTN to the tune of some $4m. It always came back to the money, and how any anti-piracy activities were to be funded.

Meanwhile the RTN reported that at a recent internal meeting, its Deputy Assistant Director of Operations had confirmed that all the relevant units had submitted their proposals, that their detailed costings would be passed up to the Operations Department within a couple of days, which would in turn submit these to the RTN Headquarters for approval, before being sent to the NSC. It was very clear that even the donation of new equipment had to follow the normal, very cautious procedures. But individuals within the RTN would sometimes suggest ways they thought might be helpful to produce results, such as the UN paying for navy personnel to become crew members on fishing boats. That idea did not catch on.

The RTN was not alone in coming up with impractical ideas. Indeed, UNHCR's staff came up with a few of their own, some of which were so absurd that I took note of them at the time. So, in addition to adjusting to the shifting agendas of the various Thai agencies, I also had to deal with this level of well-intentioned naivete from UNHCR colleagues.

(1) Perhaps it could be arranged for Thai fishing boats to shadow the refugee boats into shore, in which case there would be no need for the RTN or the Marine Police to intervene, and it might deter other Thai boats from attacking. After the refugees were safely landed and reported on the help they had received, then a reward could be paid.

(2) UNHCR could perhaps pay Thai boats if the refugees testified on arrival that here had been no rapes, no robbery, and no abductions. Provided such a scheme did not become unduly commercialised and did not go against official Thai policy, the fishermen could decide amongst themselves how to collect and share any such reward.

(3) If women and girls abducted from the boats were not thrown in the sea, instead of being sold into brothels for the reported price of US$130-220 each, perhaps agreements could be reached with the USA and the Thai Police to enable them to go straight to the USA.

(4) Perhaps Thai fishing boats could be given radios to enable them to report to a control centre when they spotted a refugee boat. The centre could note the Thai boat's registration number, the location of the refugee boats, and inform UNHCR so it could pay a reward.

Back in Songkhla, a naval officer had read a report in the Nation newspaper about the recent Granada film and was keen to express his displeasure at its criticism of the RTN. The Nation article had also cited a $5m assistance programme, so he was disappointed when I explained that the figure was just inaccurate, not a new budget. He informed me that the navy's decoy fishing boats, which were deployed at sea for 5-6 days at a time, had been moved to the edge of the continental shelf. There was still no assessment of whether they were in any way effective. Despite this, the US Consulate in Songkhla held the belief that within the limits of its experience and competence, the RTN was doing its job. This was important, since its opinion (and that of its Bangkok embassy) had a significant influence over the US State Department's attitude towards, and willingness to fund, the UNHCR's anti-piracy project.

At the Marine Police base, I was told that each province had a 50-foot patrol boat for near-shore activities, and a single 80-foot boat that had to cover the coastline from Surat Thani to the Malaysian border. The base had requested Bangkok for extended operational funds but had been given only enough for a single vessel. It had heard nothing about a new budget.

One Marine Police officer's perspective was illuminating. He thought that if the RTN were to patrol more than 100 kms from land, it would be out among the fishing fleet and would see more; that the per diem allowance that it received was less than that paid to the RTN; that any investigations it undertook were systematically leaked to the fishing boat owners by "moles" in the Harbour Department, resulting in the boats being moved to other provinces, and if any specific crew members got wind of investigations against them individually, they would jump to different boats in other ports. And he had heard from the Chairman of the Fishing Association that the RTN boats on patrol would anchor and sell fuel to fishing boats. There was no shortage of such stories to digest.

When it came to identification or arrest of individual fishermen, a further problem that the Marine Police had to face was that fishing boats under 60 tonnes usually had no crew lists. Boats over 60 tons were supposed to have them, but in reality, rarely did. Working practices on the boats were very fluid; crew members came and went depending on pay and conditions, with frequent arguments between the crew and skippers. As noted earlier, with any hint of an investigation a crew member would just jump ship, and cases had been recorded of the families of accused crew members trying to bribe the police to slow down investigations.

Despite this, attention was focussed on a live case – "Boat 0882" – a Thai fishing boat that witnesses claimed had been involved in an attack on a Vietnamese boat. The Malaysians had detained the boat and had taken photographs of all the crew members under suspicion, while in a rare example of cross-border collaboration, the Thais had arrested the boat owner pending the outcome of the investigation.

Just after New Year I was called back to Geneva to discuss progress and to review the planning for an extension of the programme for another year. Obviously, any extension would depend on both the availability of funds as well as the quality of reporting on the existing programme. The NSC had suggested (informally) that if the international community wanted the programme to continue, it should make an offer to the Thai Government, rather than the latter making a request for assistance. But, understandably, the donors preferred to be confident that the Thai Government actually wanted help. UNHCR was dancing in the middle of these sensitivities, soliciting budget details and operational reports from the agencies, and new funds from the donors.

News came in that a Vietnamese boat #2023 containing 61 people had arrived in Songkhla on 11 January 1984, from which five women had been abducted, and seven raped. Another boat of 73 people had arrived in Narathiwat near the Malaysian border after being rammed by a Thai fishing boat, and separately, 18 abductees had been found in Malaysia. So it was clear that the attacks were continuing, and I was asked to go to Kuala Lumpur to assess the latest situation there and report back. I duly returned to Bangkok, and then flew to Kuala Lumpur, where the UNHCR representative, Bayandor, told me that the Government might be interested in a regional conference to discuss piracy, but only if it were to include Vietnam (and Cambodia), the source of the boat people. The Government's legal arm had apparently said it was in favour of introducing anti-piracy legislation, but that it would take "a long time". The Malaysian Government had apparently acknowledged that Thai patrols by air or sea could enter Malaysian space – indeed, had already done so – provided that agreed procedures were adhered to. Due to the problem of Moslem separatist activities in the southern Thai provinces, the Malaysians were anxious to avoid anything that might suggest collusion with Thai Muslims.

This attitude hindered any real likelihood of joint Thai-Malaysian patrols, something that the donors were keen to encourage in pursuit of a regional approach to the issue, even if the notion of a coherent anti-piracy policy that all regional countries might agree on was a figment of donor imagination rather than a practical option. But UNHCR, pushed by its donors, was obliged to continue to explore the possibility, which I did.

23

The Donors Gather

T he proposed donor meeting loomed larger as time passed, and I was formally asked to prepare: *"a comprehensive document with a set of improved programme projects that UNHCR can move forward with and present to donor governments within the next month, assuming the Thai government will give the go-ahead to UNHCR to develop the 1984-85 programme".* This meant I had to crystallise all the information from all the agencies into a coherent proposal that would be acceptable to the shifting political concerns of the NSC.

As mentioned earlier, the good relationships that I had been able to develop gradually with officials in most of the agencies increasingly bore fruit in terms of openness and information sharing. Generally, the agencies accepted (with greater or lesser enthusiasm) that the attention of the donor countries and the activities of UNHCR were not something they could wish away. Despite the benefits of the additional equipment and funds that engagement with the programme brought them, most of them would probably have preferred not to have the programme at all, since it necessitated a whole new degree of co-ordination with other agencies and of political embroilment with central government in the shape of the NSC.

The NSC openly used the boat people and the anti-piracy programme as political footballs, and while the agencies would often be co-operative and helpful on a local level, their input was used as a card in the NSC's wider game. Everything – information, budget requests, funds – had to pass through the NSC, which routinely slowed the flow to suit its wider agenda. If it thought the USA was slackening the pace of its resettlement uptake from the camps, it would find some way to apply pressure again, often by increasing the amount of push-backs of new arrivals, by refusing meetings, by delaying reports, or by withholding permission for things to get done.

An example of this was that while the RTN in Songkhla said it was quite willing to take officials from the US Embassy out on patrol (on its donor-funded boat), it could not do so without clearance from the NSC. Another example is that I was told by officials in the Police Department that on several occasions they were prepared to have meetings with me, but that the NSC had forbidden them to have any direct contact. My co-ordination activities therefore had to include occasional (informal) lunch or dinner meetings, for which my conversational knowledge of Thai was invaluable. My RTN contacts complained privately that the Government's policy as such was made by the NSC and that "everybody was a victim of it". Its chief, Prasong, kept his cards very close to his chest and even the navy knew little about what was intended at any given time.

Geneva was insisting that before a new donors' anti-piracy meeting could be called, it was vital to arrange a meeting with the ever-elusive NSC to assess its overall reaction to the programme, to make clear the donors' continuing interest in supporting it, and to encourage Prasong to meet officials from the donor embassies and to reiterate the policy of not pushing off new boat arrivals. It was a tall order, since the Thai Government's inherent and habitual preference for flexible ambiguity made Geneva's desire for a definitive policy statement from the NSC highly unlikely.

Meanwhile the US Government continued to offer its

unflagging support for the programme. It pushed UNHCR for results, and behind the scenes encouraged the NSC to take it seriously by offering bilaterally-funded technical consultancy and coastguard training. Its positive attitude and willingness to provide funding was a great stimulus (to UNHCR), but as source of frustration since the programme inevitably moved at a slower pace than it thought desirable, largely due to the involvement of so many agencies and their respective (and unavoidable) bureaucratic procedures.

The US clearly had access to multiple sources of funds that it could apply directly, but it was nonetheless keen to ensure that the (multi-country) UNHCR programme should be (and should be seen as) the primary vehicle for international anti-piracy activities. Despite this, it was willing to offer funds direct to the Malaysian Government to encourage greater enthusiasm for anti-piracy activities.

One of the background problems was the fact that part of the Thai fishing fleet was unregistered, moved from port to port, and therefore was very difficult to trace. Another issue was that the Thais were upset that in their view the source of the problem (the flow of boat people) was not being adequately addressed, and their permanent sensitivity necessitated caution in dealing with them at every level.

The donors were keen that programme funds should be given to the Thais in instalments, with each payment dependent on reporting on activities, and to allow for modifications in operations based on local experience. The NSC of course tried to insist on full payment up-front, but the reality was that while donors initially committed funds, they paid these out over time, in part to avoid unspent amounts sitting in the NSC's accounts.

The issue of whether the donated funds were being well invested was a recurring theme of discussions with donors, and with urging from the Australians, Moussalli decided that a consultant should be hired to review the appropriateness of the equipment that the Thai agencies had procured and deployed under the programme. He asked me to draft the terms of reference for what would be a highly specific role.

1. *Considerable experience in conducting day and night air surveillance at sea and/or air-sea rescue, including exposure to the latest technology, as well as expertise in less sophisticated techniques.*
2. *Familiarity with monsoon weather conditions, ideally in the South China Sea.*
3. *Practical knowledge of a wide range of communications equipment used in aircraft and wooden and metal hulled-ships for linkage with land-based units with both fixed and portable equipment.*
4. *Focus on the compatibility of equipment already in use with that on order to make recommendations to the most effective deployment.*
5. *If the expert(s) were to be from the armed forces, someone with direct commercial knowledge of equipment currently in the market should be included to advise on whether the proposed items were the best option available within the constraints of the budget.*

As the Australians were reluctant to been seen as the instigator of the review (due to that fear of upsetting the Thais again), UNHCR was expected to negotiate with the RTG on the donors' behalf, which meant having to overcome the inevitable initial resistance to the idea. It was generally recognised that funding was most likely to be provided by the US (which it duly was).

Uncorroborated reports from the field indicated that the attacks were continuing: a boat of 15 was believed to have left

Vietnam on 1st April, and had been attacked with only one survivor; a boat of 44 had left Vietnam on 10th April, from which 3 girls had been abducted before it had been sunk, one survivor; another boat of 30 had left Vietnam on the 10th, from which 3 girls had been abducted, it had been pushed off from Thailand and landed in Malaysia; two more boats, containing 26 and 17 people respectively, had landed in Malaysia also after being repulsed from Thailand; and a boat of 42 had left Vietnam on 19th April, with 3 girls abducted en route. All these stories had to be checked out, but the information was circulating in the camps and among the people working in them.

Informal feedback from the donors suggested they would refuse any further commitment of funds without seeing financial reports on how much was left unspent from the existing programme. The Danes were keen to know whether the Thai Government had made a formal request for the programme to continue, the Dutch wanted to know more about the co-ordination efforts, the Norwegians thought there was too much emphasis on capital investment rather than operations, while the Germans thought that the programme had become a lot more political than before, and that more effective monitoring was required to ensure its humanitarian intent still applied.

Finally on May 11, UNHCR convened a formal meeting of the donors in Geneva, which attracted 5 officials from the US, 2 from each of the UK, Japan, Australia, and Canada, and sole representatives from Switzerland, the Netherlands, Germany, and the ICRC (the International Red Cross) as an observer. In addition to the Regional Anti-Piracy Co-ordinator, UNHCR had a heavyweight presence which included Moussalli as Head of the Protection Division, and the High Commissioner himself, who opened the meeting by emphasising that while the programme exceeded UNHCR's normal activities, he believed it to be extremely worthwhile and that it should be continued, even if its effectiveness could be questioned.

– The USA was strongly in support, offered an additional US$1.5m for a new programme in addition to its bilateral assistance, and thought that any idea of buying a new boat should be considered separately from the main programme.

– The Australians stated that their support would be maintained at a level not less than the previous year, but that a formal pledge would be made at a later date. Although it felt that too much emphasis had been given so far to equipment purchase rather than operations, they were in broad support of the programme and agreed with the USA that co-ordination between the Thai agencies should be improved. They were keen to see a more rigorous monitoring mechanism, but that it should be "carefully handled for fear of giving the impression of excessive scrutiny".

– The Canadians expressed their shock at the recent statistics for attacks on boats, thought that the suppression forces should have a more visible presence on land and at sea, and that prosecutions of perpetrators should be stepped up. Their overall attitude was "very positive" but they wanted to see assurances at the highest level that the Thai Government was committed to the programme. Nonetheless, they felt that funding should be continued.

– The Norwegians stated that their government was prepared to support the programme's continuation, perhaps at a higher level of funding, and that in their view the quality of reporting had improved.

– The Germans emphasised their view that a greater number of smaller boats should be deployed rather than fewer, larger, vessels, and that the land component (co-ordination between agencies, arrests, and prosecutions) was the most important aspect.

– The UK supported the programme's intention and its uninterrupted continuation but thought that there would be difficulties to do this without Thai assurances that the push-backs would cease, so that any future pledging would likely be conditional on this. It fully understood the sensitivities of maintaining an effective monitoring system and would endorse this, since the prime objective was to help the RTG become more effective.

– The Japanese hoped the programme would continue, and that any new proposals would be studied in Tokyo. They were concerned about cost-effectiveness, supported periodic monitoring reports, and underlined the importance of maintaining good relations with the Thais.

– The Swiss were generous enough to thank UNHCR for its efforts to date. They were aware of the difficulties involved, thought that improvements had been made, hoped that more reports would be forthcoming, and that the Swiss Government would continue its support.

– The Netherlands stated that it was not yet in a position to express a positive view, so would not give any new pledges. It wanted to assess the effectiveness of the new proposals, what other donors were going to do, and the extent to which the RTG was prepared to co-operate at a higher level.

– The ICRC, true to its habitual haughty tone, said that in its view the efficiency of the Thai agencies had yet to be demonstrated, that push-backs were unacceptable, and that funding amounts needed to be more precise.

The High Commissioner closed the meeting by noting what he appeared to think had been the "encouraging response" and by underlining that the APP was not, and could not be, part of the UNHCR's regular programme in Thailand. Moussalli would go to Bangkok later in the month to negotiate the programme's extension on the basis of working out "modalities for greater government effectiveness" and establishing more regular monitoring and reporting. He also cautioned that the Thai Prime Minister Prem Tinsulanonda, and the Foreign Minister Siddhi Savetsila, were both "very much against" the programme. This helped to put UNHCR's – and my own – efforts in context.

A couple of weeks later, Moussalli did indeed turn up in Bangkok and, with the Regional Representative Jacques Terlin, an old-school Belgian administrator-type, hosted a meeting with the donor embassies, whose representatives echoed the sentiments that their colleagues had expressed in Geneva. The following day, we met officials from the US Embassy. As usual, they had practical suggestions as to how things might be improved – for example, perhaps the RTN could lease a new vessel rather than buy one to avoid the lengthy construction period? (The RTN did not agree to this). The US observed that the recent arrests of fishermen had had a good impact abroad and that more prosecutions should be encouraged.

They added that if it were not for Prasong (the head of the NSC), there would have been no arrests. His style (as noted earlier) was not to signal what he was doing, and especially not to foreigners, and he usually did far more than they realised. He was due to visit Europe and the UK in the near future and should therefore be encouraged and supported rather than criticised. The US view was that Prasong was basically supportive of the programme, but hated to be lectured to, and "occasionally did irrational things" (such as encourage push-backs if, or whenever, the countries of resettlement were thought to be easing up on the numbers they accepted from the camps). To my mind, nothing that Prasong did was irrational, but rather the fruit of a highly intelligent and strategic mind that always prioritised Thailand's interests.

The US was concerned that the UNHCR's anti-piracy effort

was under-staffed, and therefore offered to place someone in its Bangkok office. The proposed placement had worked in Danang for 14 years, and was apparently known and held in high regard by the US refugee bureau. It was made clear that such a person "should have the confidence of the US Embassy", and be someone who "would have empathy towards, and know when and how to speak with Thais". This person was to be Carl B. Harris, whom we will meet later.

The following day, we had a meeting with Prasong and Sawat, one of his NSC deputies. Moussalli passed on the High Commissioner's greetings and support, said that the recent arrests had been very well received, that more would be appreciated, and that he understood that results depended on funding. Prasong complained about the funding delays, since any delays "made the agencies unhappy", even claiming that the RTN wanted to pull out of the programme because of the lack of money (a view that was not consistent with my discussions with them). He was upset that Thailand was seen by the press and the international community as being responsible for the attacks (which of course it was not, even if some of its citizens were).

Moussalli conveyed the donors' view that better reporting and evidence of greater operational effectiveness was desirable, stating that US$2m could be made available the following month (June), with the rest following soon thereafter. Prasong undertook to find out the agencies' immediate needs, said that he knew the right tactics to ensure their co-operation, but cautioned that he had enemies "inside" to fight as well. He promised to look into the most efficient ways for producing the reports that were being asked for. And on that note the high-level meetings ended. Moussalli returned to Geneva, seemingly satisfied that the programme was on the right track and that crucial relationships were sound.

While this was true, it was far from the whole picture. In the provinces, there was still a lot of ignorance about the programme and how it worked, to the extent that on several occasions I had to suggest to the local police that they could claim (for example) a share of the budget for information gathering. There were also signs that the programme was in danger of being taken over by Government bureaucracy, since the Ministry of Interior was trying to take a more active "supervisory" role that would necessitate the provincial governors being put in charge of anti-piracy activities in their respective provinces. For this it had apparently drawn up a project that would involve district offices and villages and require the Police Department to report every month. It was clear that the operating agencies did not want this added source of potential interference, and (fortunately) I never had to include the MoI in my co-ordination activities.

The agency co-ordination centre, the idea of which was widely supported by the donors, was supposed to be operating out of Songkhla, but inter-agency rivalry meant that it functioned in name only. The RTN was very conscious of security and liked to keep its activities secret. It said that the Police kept asking it to share its plans, which it did not want to do as it thought it would compromise its strategy and it had no confidence in the police's ability to maintain confidentiality. The Police Department was a civilian entity that focussed on crime suppression; the RTN's priorities were military and national security. Neither wanted to get too involved with the other.

Meanwhile, the agencies in the provinces were asking whether UNHCR could procure the new equipment directly from abroad, and hand it over, rather than them having to make requests through the NSC and wait for months for its procurement rules to be followed. It was a good idea that, in principle, I favoured, but given the practical realities would never have worked. The stated reason was that both sides should have a single point of contact for negotiations and control, and any direct procurement by and delivery to the agencies would have undermined the government's centralised operating model. Furthermore, it would have been impossible for UNHCR to get into the business of buying equipment that could (or would very likely) have military use.

24

The Germans Intervene

Shortly afterwards, the German Ambassador, Herr Lankes, visited the RTN Songkhla base, accompanied by an official from the Canadian Embassy. The meeting, hosted by three senior Thai naval officers, offered an interesting clash of cultures. Herr Lankes opened by asking what improvements had been made (as a result of the programme), said that the USA was pushing his government to persist with its support, but that without "noticeable changes", the current programme would be the last that Germany would participate in.

Captain Manon was forthright in his response, emphasising the RTN's inability to patrol international waters, and recalling a recent incident where a Thai fishing boat had been seen attacking a refugee boat but had fled the scene when the RTN patrol flight had flown over. He claimed that there had been two incidents of Vietnamese attacking Thai fishing boats, in which one Thai skipper had been killed. 75% of such attacks took place in Vietnamese, Malaysian, or international waters, where Thais could not make arrests. The "extreme efforts" of the Thai Government were not well publicised, and anyway the Vietnamese should not directly or indirectly encourage the boat people to leave. (To me, this last comment sounded as though it had come straight out of the NSC's strategy book).

Manon repeated the RTN's need for a new large patrol boat, thought that the Harbour Department's installation of a new computer would "improve the performance of the anti-piracy unit", and that "more energetic pursuit" on the part of the Land and Marine Police would lead to prosecutions.

While Herr Lankes agreed with Manon's views on Vietnam, he did not see what the two incidents referred to had to do with the anti-piracy programme. The attacks had obviously been made by Vietnamese naval vessels and it was misleading to call them pirates. The programme's "enemy" was not official patrol craft, but individual private boats. Manon then quoted a (local?) convention that any incident involving robbery, rape or attack could be termed piracy.

Captain Somboon tried to clarify the issue by saying that Thai trawlers had been attacked 40 miles off the Camau peninsula, within the 50-mile fishery protection zone that The Vietnamese had recently declared. They had seized a Thai trawler which had apparently asked for help (from the RTN) but that it had not been possible to respond to the call (apparently due to a lack of suitable boats).

The Canadian representative then piped up to ask whether the RTN would offer assistance in the event there were other such attacks and wondered what the donor response might be if such activity was presented as being a major component of the programme, as opposed to preventing attacks on Vietnamese refuge boats.

Herr Lankes was "amazed" that such incidents should be presented as part of the programme, and strongly advised that they should be taken out of any future presentation. Bonn was already hesitant about its support, but this would likely intensify if it thought that assistance was being offered to Thai boats.

Captain Manoon explained that they had cited the incident to show that the small coastal patrol craft provided by the programme were too small to be of use at a distance, and that a larger vessel (like the model requested under the proposed new programme) was more suitable. His colleague Captain Somboon quickly added that while the APP was the primary role of the programme, the RTN's secondary role was to offer assistance to all vessels.

Herr Lankes pressed on relentlessly. Why were so few boats being examined? Wouldn't searching every boat that came back into port be an efficient and visible means of deterrent? Somboon replied that the RTN could not (i.e., would not) hamper or harass normal fishing activities, and that they would search only suspected boats. Search methods that were too heavy-handed would be seen, and criticised, by Thais as "anti-civic action".

Despite the clear differences of perspective and robust exchanges, the meeting ended calmly enough, and I took the party over to see the camp, which had its usual stimulative effect on visitors. The ambassador was very active, surrounded by curious children, many suffering from skin disease, and asked numerous questions both of the refugees and of a visibly embarrassed Deputy Governor, who I was able to help by fielding some of the questions. After the visit, the ambassador declared that he would recommend to his diplomatic colleagues that an ambassador should go down on every inspection trip. This, he thought, would be excellent for visibility and would allow more "high profile enquires" to be made.

He also thought that it would be a good idea to pay a visit to the Harbour Department in Bangkok to check on progress. So, since I had offered to accompany him, ten days later Ambassador Lankes appeared in UNHCR's office bearing a letter he had received from the RTN in Songkhla after his visit there. He shared the contents with us and while I don't recall exactly what the letter said, I did make a note of Jacques Terlin's reaction: he thought the RTN were "either very stupid or very childish". Clearly, great offence had been taken at the ambassador's undiplomatic approach, and I would have to smooth ruffled naval feathers when I next went down to Songkhla. I feared the worst for our imminent meeting at the Harbour Department.

In fact, it went better than I had expected. Amphorn Triyabhon, the Deputy Director General, was well prepared, and the ambassador had toned down his aggression, perhaps chastened by the reaction to his visit to Songkhla. Amphorn briefed us that the Director General had refused to accept the Wang computer delivered under the programme for the registration process as it had been the wrong model, but that a new machine was on the way. A Chulalongkorn University professor was completing a study into the registration system, to be delivered the following month, and the Harbour Department had applied to the Civil Service Commission for additional staff to be trained to handle the registration process.

Herr Lankes began his interrogation: how long would the registration take? Six months, Amphorn thought. And the department had all the power it needed for the job? Definitely. It might take up to a year for all the provincial offices to be oriented, as it was "difficult to train some provincial staff". The ambassador said that his government was hesitant to support the programme further since it had received much criticism, and appeared to suffer from administrative chaos, so before any discussion of a new budget, it would be good to see tangible results in the form of pirates being apprehended and the number of attacks reduced. He would need to be personally convinced that progress was being made and would want to look at the parts of the programme that emphasised deterrence.

Amphorn thanked him for his opinion and agreed that to date a "proper organisation for fighting piracy" had been wanting. The agencies involved had been going out on patrol independently, which in his opinion was useless, and there was a lack of co-operation, especially in the south. He noted that there were some 25,000 fishing boats to register, and that "the fish around here all belong to our neighbours". He added that the transfer of existing boat registrations to the new electronic system would make research and tracking much quicker, and it could only get better with (on the condition of) better co-operation with the other agencies involved. He was setting up a new department to handle this and was also trying to establish a register of seamen to contain their biodata and addresses.

The ambassador seemed satisfied with this, and after the meeting, which ended amicably, was certainly better informed about the role of the Harbour Department in the programme as a facilitator rather than as an agent of suppression.

25

Consolidation

When I got back to the office, a Thai colleague, Choosin, had just returned from a meeting with the Police, who had received reports of (or more likely, already knew about) "floating brothels" that served the Thai fishing fleet at sea. They had investigated to find out whether they may have had Vietnamese women on board and had seemingly been relieved to confirm that the unfortunate girls were in fact from Isan (the Northeast). This might have been positive news were it not for the fact that we knew that many or most abducted Vietnamese women were either thrown in the sea after they had outlived their usefulness or sold as slaves into brothels on the mainland. It also begged the question of whether the Isan girls were on the boats out of choice or because they had been trafficked. It was a grim business in any case.

The commercial aspects of the programme were continuing to suffer from the habitually frustrating negotiations between Hawker Pacific (the supplier of the Nomad aircraft) and the RTN. The latter wanted to have a full 360-degree radar fitted to the new planes, instead of the 270-degree radar that had been installed. If the RTN got its way, Hawker Pacific would have to do the fitting (at considerable extra cost), which to them seemed otiose, given that the RTN already had a Fokker F-28 fully kitted out with complete maritime surveillance equipment, including 360-degree radar. (When asked about it, the RTN said that it could only be used for national defence purposes, not anti-piracy).

Since the southern coastal provinces were involved in the programme, I decided to make a trip down to Songkhla by road, calling in at the police headquarters in the key provincial capitals along the way. In Chumphon, Surat, and Nakon Sri Thammarat therefore, I held meetings with the National and Marine Police, mainly to inform them that the programme existed, and that there was a budget for such things as basic equipment such as radios, and information gathering. The reaction was mixed, one of curiosity rather than hostility.

It was clear that attacks on Vietnamese boats were very low on their list of priorities, and it turned out that the police did not use the word piracy. Such programme-related activity that occurred was seemingly co-ordinated by the regional police headquarters, which had to submit their plans to the provincial governors, which in turn submitted these to Bangkok and the NSC. It was a tortuous path.

The result was that nobody at ground level was very interested, did not know what the strategy was, how much budget was available, or what they were supposed to do. In most cases it was very little, since what little activity that did occur (and related budget spend) was centred on the main fishing ports of Surat, Nakon Sri Thammarat, and Songkhla. It was a sobering and instructive trip and underlined the limited extent of the programme's reach.

The issue of additional staff was still being pushed by the US, and it was being made clear that its support for the programme would necessitate the hiring of the official it had proposed. To prepare for this, Geneva asked me to work out the most appropriate allocation of staff for the programme. This was not a complicated task – two people in Bangkok and one in Songkhla, or one in each of Bangkok, Songkhla, and

Malaysia? In the end, since only one new person was to be added, and it would have been unwise to let him roam around unsupervised, I decided that he should be based in Bangkok with me.

His job description duly drafted and approved, Carl B. Harris arrived a short time later, a fair-haired middle-aged man with a crew cut, and an endearing habit of blushing intensely. This made him an immediate target of good-natured teasing in the office, where he was quickly accepted as a new member of the team. He had a good heart, was well-intentioned, even if sometimes naïve in his view of the world, and often shocked by some of what he came across. His initial presence in some of his early meetings with the agencies created new tensions, since he was clearly seen as having been planted by the Americans to keep an eye on their activities. But he was acutely aware of this, and while he therefore took some time to adjust to the realities of the world of anti-piracy, over time he became a valuable ally in handling the issues that arose and being able to feed back to the US Embassy information on what the UNHCR (and indeed, the agencies) were doing, which was often more than it believed.

26

The net closes

After nearly a year on the job, I had managed to create a web of information and communication that had become quite effective and that covered all the distinct groups: the donor governments, the Thai agencies, UNHCR offices in the region and at headquarters, and within the Bangkok office itself. The donor governments all had direct access to senior UNHCR officials either in Bangkok or in Geneva if they wanted it, but the less formal working level contacts that I established with each of them were generally more useful and could be off the record.

Traditionally, the Thai agencies had had minimal experience of having to collaborate with other agencies, and this posed a definite problem. Each one was vertically siloed and strictly hierarchical, whereby any issue or communication at or from an operating level had to be sent up the line to an appropriate higher level, which would communicate with its counterpart in a different agency at a similar level, before being transmitted down to the operating level of that agency for action to be taken or for the information to be shared. It was slow, inefficient, and often creatively obstructive.

My arrival on the scene eventually allowed for instant cross-agency communication, in that I could, and did, just get in touch with my contacts in the relevant agencies to find something out or to share information. Each agency came to realise that this could cut corners and time, and so became a valuable element in making progress. Obviously, it took some time to establish the necessary level of trust, and once it was in place, I was very careful to protect it.

Communication with UNHCR colleagues was a different challenge. I reported directly to the Director of Protection in Geneva, Moussalli, and to the people working under him. I had to keep the head of the Bangkok office informed about what I was doing and had to attend meetings that he would occasionally have with the ambassadors of the donor countries. I also had to work with the legal department in the Bangkok office, which was responsible for following up on individual cases and for protection issues in the camps, and with the resettlement team, who handled the ongoing flow of people from the camps to third countries. I was also in regular touch with (giving and receiving information, and visiting occasionally) the UNHCR representatives in Malaysia, Indonesia, and (to a lesser extent) the Philippines. Finally, I also had to keep the Public Information team informed, since many of the requests for information it received were to do with the programme.

It was a stimulating role, since at any time I knew more about the programme than almost anyone else, and so became a key point of contact for anyone who wanted to find out about what was going on. This is not to say that I knew much about what was going on in each of the agencies, clearly I didn't, but what I knew was much more than the heads of the agencies were prepared to divulge in official meetings with UNHCR or donor governments. And it also meant that, understandably, I was pestered incessantly by everybody in the web, either looking for information or asking me for funds, or to intervene to get something (a report, a budget) unblocked.

As one of his first tasks, Carl thought it would be a good idea to create a map of what he called the "bureaucratic complexities" of the anti-piracy programme, showing all the reporting channels and information flows. He duly presented a remarkably detailed and accurate map, which unfortunately I did not keep a copy of.

Little by little, the operational aspects of the programme were improving, egged on by the temptation of new capital and operating funds from donors (and particularly under continuous pressure from the US Government which ensured that the Thai Government took it more seriously than they would probably have liked). Donors were, justifiably, always asking for evidence of 'implementation effectiveness', and the need for adequate reporting was an endless feature of discussions with the NSC and the agencies.

Meanwhile, the programme continued. In early September, the Australians were to hand over two new Nomad aircraft to the RTN, to be equipped with the Ercisson SLAR (Sideways Looking Airborne Radar) that was thought to be appropriate for the task of identifying refugee and fishing boats. Such bilateral (military) assistance from both the Australian and US Governments meant that the RTN understood well that although there was no official link, it had to be seen to be co-operating seriously with the anti-piracy programme.

Another aspect of bilateral assistance was the anti-narcotic programme that the US Government invested in through the NSC. It already had six intelligence-gathering teams up and down the country in Thailand, and it was suggested that these could be used to help gather information on pirate activity as well (even though the Thais claimed, unsurprisingly, that it was "difficult" to find willing informers). The NSC thought that to avoid confusion, any such initiative should come through UNHCR, and that any resulting information should be channelled through UNHCR.

With the US Government insisting that it wanted to set up

a special programme to be staffed by its own people, it was relatively easy to sidestep this idea, since it would inevitably have led to conflicts between the programmes. Narcotics was an international crime issue that involved Interpol, while attacks refugee boats were, relatively speaking, a very minor issue, and the Marine Police and the RTN were already operating a nominal information-gathering activity under the existing programme.

The link between the Marine Police and the Harbour Department was by this time operating much more quickly than before – information on boat registrations was now being given "almost instantaneously", and a list of boats to be detained and inspected was handed to the RTN. In addition information from UNHCR"s offices in Malaysia on suspected pirate attacks was being transmitted very rapidly for follow up action.

Among the agencies, there was a growing realisation that patrolling the high seas was an inefficient way of operating. The RTN could not harass or investigate fishing boats without justification, decoy boats were useless, and successful prosecutions were in fact the most effective way of getting the message across that pirates could be caught and punished. The Thai Marine Police had started to take photographs of boats alleged to be involved in attacks, and these were being shown for identification to surviving refugees in both Thailand and Malaysia. This information was then shared with the Thai Police so it could begin its investigations.

It was a long and slow process, but reports suggested that some word of this was beginning to spread among the fishing communities. Not that the attacks stopped, but at least there was a wider awareness that something was being done. And even the Thai Government could begin to see that its international standing was improved by its apparent, if half-hearted, efforts to stamp out the violence against the refugees.

I had originally signed up for a one-year assignment and before the time was up, I agreed to an extension of some months in order to get to a point where I could be confident that the programme was in satisfactory order and functioning reasonably effectively. In addition, Carl's arrival implied a period of transition since it would take some time for him to settle in, learn to temper his instincts, and thereby avoid unnecessary complications. There was also the question of finding someone to replace me.

I referred earlier to the information and communication web that I had painstakingly built up and had been managing, but this – inevitably I suppose – became over time a net that I felt increasingly ensnared in. It was a dynamic construct that fluctuated all the time, depending on external and local events, the individuals involved, the requests for funds, the immediacy of problems, et al. It was a lot to keep on top of, and while a working knowledge of Thai and an understanding of Thai culture had been essential in creating it, there was the ever-present danger of being sucked too far into the Thai orbit.

On one of my frequent visits to Geneva, Moussalli asked whether I would return to the organisation after the assignment. I told him that I had long harboured an ambition to get into the private sector, and that if I didn't do it then, it might be too late. His response was that I should follow my instincts, which I subsequently did, and therefore never enquired further about possible new positions with UNHCR, nor indeed were any offered to me.

As so often happens, and to emphasise the truism that no one is irreplaceable, a suitable candidate to take over the Regional Anti-Piracy Co-ordinator's role appeared in due course. Robin, a tall, easy-going, fluent Thai-speaking New Zealander, married to a Thai, with an impressive ability to sing Thai folk songs, had been in Thailand long enough to be sensitive to Thai ways and to know how to get around them. As far as I was concerned, he was well suited to the role, and I could leave with a clear conscience.

As I made the rounds of the agencies to say my farewells and introduce my successor, the Thai individuals I had got to know quite well were all generous in their tributes, the Naval Captain in charge of the Songkhla naval station even going so far as to say that he had never met a more effective co-ordinator. It was much appreciated, even if I was in all probability the only foreign co-ordinator he had ever come across. The Bangkok UNHCR office staff were all very kind and said the right things, and I left with a sense that I had been able to define more clearly and develop the imprecise role I had taken on, had established a functional system to underpin it, and that there were new people to take it forward.

· 27 ·

Looking Back

I n 2005, a major conference was held in the UK on the future of the *UN Convention on the Status of Refugees. Part of its report* noted that:

> *In 1951, no one anticipated that the process of refugee determination would become institutionalised. It was not foreseen that there would be a requirement of due process by virtue of which the claimant would have a right, expectation, or entitlement to advice and legal representation ... The drafters of the 1951 Convention did not consider that decision-making would be anything but discretionary by an enlightened administration but without their being hampered by the requirements of due process as we understand them.*

Over the past few decades, the system that was devised 70 years ago to deal with fewer than one million European refugees within Europe has, very evidently, become unviable in a modern age which offers connections and communication systems – mobile phones, the internet, television, social media, mass air travel – far beyond the imaginations of the enlightened people that set up the 1951 Convention. Despite the intervening decades of thousands of people learning how to manipulate the system to their benefit, and an entire industry and well-organised criminal organisations emerging and flourishing on the spoils it provides, the Convention remains unaltered and seemingly sacrosanct. The report went on:

> *The principal beneficiaries of current international refugee administration are immigration lawyers, migration agents, and – above all – people smugglers. This ... benefits a tiny portion of the millions of refugees around the globe... those with sufficient money to be able to get to the West while the tens of millions of real refugees languish in refugee camps with no hope of ever being offered asylum.*

The seeds of these basic issues elaborated at the conference had already been sown in my mind when I closed the door on the UNHCR in 1985. The issues have become infinitely greater today, but it was clear even during my time in UNHCR that no matter how hard I worked or how effective I could be, while immediate problems could be resolved, the ongoing issues never went away, and in many ways could be said to have worsened. The problem of the boat people dragged on for many more years, with the last camp in Malaysia closed only in 2001. The anti-piracy programme ran on until 1991, and two years later the last camp in Thailand for Laotians was closed. The official UNHCR report on the events of that time[24] briefly summarises – and contextualises – the period and the events I have related in these pages.

For the first four years in Thailand, I had spent most of the time working and living largely on my own, frequently in challenging settings that only I had been witness to, and usually without anybody to whom I could turn for instant advice.

---

24. See Appendix 3 – extract from the UNHCR report "State of the World's Refugees 2000". The full report makes interesting – if dispassionate - reading and provides more detail for anyone looking for additional information.

I therefore had become accustomed to having to take decisions knowing that I would have to live with both the consequences of the decisions, and with myself. Almost every day, morning and night, I had had to look at my reflection in the mirror and ask myself whether the decisions I had made and the actions I had taken had been to the best of my ability and judgement in the circumstances. It was an inescapable daily routine that left no wriggle room – my conscience became my only guide to whether I had lived up to both the standards that I set for myself, as well as those I had absorbed or had been imprinted on me from an early age. But all were exposed to regular and rigorous testing.

The factual reports that I filed with the head office provided the necessary information of any incident, but were only partial accounts as they did not, nor could they, describe the moral or emotional context in which the incident had arisen. The issues that I had to wrestle with were not subject to any official code of conduct, but were the result of inner motivations that forced me to answer questions of whether, in each situation, I had made enough effort, or invested enough time, or acted with enough courage, or shown enough commitment, or enough compassion, or demonstrated the best example of what I thought the organisation represented, or acted in the most honest and professional manner. In short, I quickly worked out that the only way to survive in a healthy state and to be effective was always to be as true to myself as possible. And it was something that I tried to adhere to thereafter.

I acknowledge that I was very fortunate in my time in the UN, enjoying an unusual degree of freedom of initiative, action and movement, and deriving great satisfaction from most of the work, especially that in the field. But I was also increasingly aware that I lacked (or perhaps was reluctant to develop) some of the skills that I thought I would need to make a successful long-term career in the UN, and could see that any such bureaucratic system was, and would be, frustrating.

Through luck and good timing, and without any personal backing, I had found a way into the organisation when it was still quite small, and I had been privileged to enjoy a short run of interesting and challenging posts in which I had had remarkable autonomy. I had met and worked with some very fine, courageous, and honourable people. Also, inevitably, with others of lesser quality. But throughout, there had been a palpable and worthy *esprit de corps* among colleagues that it was a privilege to have been part of.

Nearly all my working life up to this point, albeit rich in experience, had been within just one UN agency, a significant but nonetheless small part of the overall UN organisation, itself a pool of privilege in the wide ocean of life. I knew I needed a wider exposure to life, and the private sector lured me on towards its very different set of difficulties, rigours, and rewards.

But that is another story, perhaps for another time.

Appendix 1

Statement by Thai Thieu Viet, a Vietnamese refugee who arrived in Thailand on 1 April 1978. Passed to me in the camp after his arrival.

"Either Die or Live Free"

"Rather die than live without freedom". This very practical and meaningful old Chinese proverb has just been an overwhelming inner force and courage which has moved us, 51 Vietnamese refugees, to abandon all our possessions and assets, to risk our lives, to escape out of Communist Vietnam and to look for freedom.

"We, 51 refugees, including 26 boys and girls, 14 women (two of them 8 months pregnant) and 11 men, belonging to six separate families, planned and scheduled to purchase a 16 meter wooden boat, used only for transferring passengers and cargoes on interior rivers, in order to venture across the sea to search for freedom.

"Since the boat was not an ocean or sea-ship, it was easily mistaken at many checkpoints of the ... (*illegible*) at the river gate called GANH HAO at CA-MAU province of South Vietnam ...... the "stop" flashlight signal, whistles and gunshots of the Communist police at the gate. After only 15 minutes from the gate, we unfortunately hit a shallow sandbank. The gate police did not know, so we all jumped into the water and pushed the boat away from the shore. The, according to the compass, we steered the boat, heading 230°, intending to reach Thailand or Malaysia.

"On the second day, about 06.00 on 30 March 1978, we saw five communist fishing ships chasing after us. They threatened us so much that we made up our minds to make a dead race with them. God blessed and, thanks to our obedient engine, we managed to leave the communist ships far behind and so they had to give up their intention of chasing and arresting us.

"Due to long hours of high-speed running, the water began to get in through the propellor shaft at the rear. We had all, alternately and unceasingly, to exhaust our energy by pouring out the water which got in so quickly; still, it didn't help and the situation became worse, until about 03.00 on 31st March. We thought we might all be drowned, yet we struggled on till 20.00 on that date, when I saw a Thailand fishing boat. The Thailand ship came to the rescue, getting all women and children over the ship, and tugged our boat behind, leaving all our men and some of the ship's crew to continue pouring water out (bailing). After 15 hours the boat was unsalvageable, it began to sink so we had to let it go.

"We were rescued on to a seashore of Thailand called Laem Dachi and we were told to wait for the Thai police to settle us. When the Thai ship left, we waited from 08.00 of 1st April to 21.00, when we were sleeping on the shore and were robbed by five men carrying axes and knives.

"However around 15.00, 1st April we encountered a group of Pattani University students having a picnic on the beach. We asked them to do the favour for us of reporting to the local police our incident. They promised that they would by the next day, when they had returned to Pattani. They supplied us with food and water and even gave us all the food they would have had for their morning breakfast.

"13.00 of 2nd April the robbers came again for their greedy

search, so we decided to leave the place and walked for miles to a navy lamp tower where we stayed for the night.

"09.00 of 3rd April 78, we were finally picked up by the Thailand (Pattani) official personnel and security officers who had gone through our names and every detail required. They settled us at a small fishing village where we have received the most generous hospitality which made us temporarily forget we are miserable and pitiful refugees.

"On the 4th April there came some lecturers plus some Pattani university students whom we met days ago. They brought us boxes of food, medicines, rice, charcoal, some daily necessities and 45 in Thai money which had been distributed by good hearted Christians. We conversed for hours and had all our names, date and place of birth, nationalities, relationships, occupations, education, filled in on a paper form. Of course, we all felt so touched by their charity, their assistance, and their care. I represented our group in expressing our deep and sincere gratitude towards them and did not forget to send our best regards and thanks.

"Today, the 5th of April '78, I woke up early, sitting on the beach, looking at the sun rising from the East and listening to the roaring of the wavs of the sea. For the first time after running away from Vietnam I felt so safe, at ease, and delight-fully excited while I was thinking that from this moment on, I will be able to breathe the real "free air" of life. With the assistance and effort of the Thai Government, my family and I and also the whole group of refugees might immigrate into Australia or the USA etc.

"If it were not for Communism, Vietnam could be a good place to live. The weather is S. Vietnam has never been too cold, although sometimes it would be a little hot, the oriental people could easily get used to it. Besides the land is so fertile, green trees could be seen all year round, the rice grows richly, fish are numerous and fat. In short, to earn a living in south Vietnam is very easy as long as one is willing to work, and one gets rich if one has a good brain and strives hard.

"Before the communists got the south, it was President Nguyen Van Thieu who ran the government when, no matter what race, people would be allowed to do all kinds of businesses and occupations as long as taxes were paid and they were legal. People "harvested" what they really worked hard for, and they enjoyed their lives because they had been protected by the "rights' contributed by the laws.

"Under the President Thieu Government everybody might breather "free air", people lived wherever they liked to, ran any business they thought appropriate, kept their earned money either in the bank or in their house as they desired; free worship of religion; they lived happily and saw the laws properly maintained.

"Then the communists came, we lost our freedom, lost the meaning of life, which is, indeed, a most broken-hearted and regretful thing. It is not the time for us to find out whose fault it was, and who to blame, for the loss of the country to the communists.

"People have heard of and scared of communists yet, as a refugee from communism, with personal experience, I should realise well enough how terrible communism is; and so one feels threatened even just hearing of communism, like one turns pale on hearing of a fearful tiger.

"The communists had won South Vietnam because they made use of the less educated, poor, poor people who could be easily tamed by the sweet promises of communism. Like a starved person when he is told where he may get food and treasure, he will certainly try his best efforts to get them. Therefore, comparing the South Vietnamese soldiers with the

North Vietnamese soldiers' desire and earnestness of fighting, we could tell who would win and who would lose.

"Communism allows no private assets, no merchants, only the farmers who grow rice and vegetables ae respected; secondly, the workers who manufacture clothing and daily necessities area also deemed necessary. Students would learn nothing but the communist theories. They spent most of their time hoeing the farms in the fields, in cleaning the streets, in forcing the businessmen to close their shops and to search a new life in some uncultivated land far from the cities, which they called "New Economic Zones". With unreasonable excuses they forced people out of the houses where they moved in to live.

"The rich people would automatically be listed in the names of the "guilty" because they were considered to have "squeezed" the poor people's "Sweat and blood". They were gradually put in jail and everything they had was confiscated. The ordinary, not rich merchants would be concerned about the government's high taxes and would close their shops, waiting the day of the end of the world. The poor people worry the most because of unemployment and high cost of living.

"The only portion of the people who might live in cities were those who worked for government factories and government organisations. They would get the lowest pay, which was not even able to pay off their breakfast every morning. And yet they had to work without scheduled hours and attend all kinds of conferences and meetings. Also, every family should go off to boring meetings every evening.

"The engine needs gas and oil to turn well; the buffalo needs food and good health to plough the fields well; it has been only the communists who have forced people to work unrestingly and caring nothing for their stomachs.

"People sooner or later see through it and realise the communist promises are "poison wrapped in candy dress" which once anyone takes them will surely die. Therefore, people began and continue to escape from the communist Vietnamese, through the "iron curtain" to search for freedom. We are only a (small) number of refugees among the whole. People would rather risk their lives in running away than live and suffer communism. The fact is that we may always listen to the radio broadcasts of foreign countries about ships and refugees being rescued by Thailand, Malaysia, Japan, Philippines, Australia, even Norway etc. and they have gradually been immigrated into Australia or the USA.

"I myself as a refugee, first of all would thank so much the Thailand Government, Thai people and good-hearted foreigners who have been so kind, courteous and generous in rescuing us, supplying food, assisting us to get our will fulfilled so that we may soon live in the free country, like USA, Australia, Canada etc. as we wish. At last, I wish the Thailand King and Queen as well as the free Thai nation long life forever!"

Thailand, 5th April 1978.

Vietnamese refugee Thai Thieu Viet,
(Discharged V. N. Airforce Airtraffic controller)

Appendix 2

Source: https://history.state.gov/historicaldocuments/frus1977-80v22/d148

Telegram from the US Embassy in Thailand to the Department of State
Bangkok, December 30, 1980, 0924Z

Subj: Motivations of Vietnamese Boat Refugees.

The following message on Vietnamese refugees is from Am-Consul Songkhla. Also transmitted is a comment and different perspective on the problem from the Embassy's refugee section. Both are introduced by an Embassy comment.

A. Embassy Introduction

There are no sure answers to the question of what motivates the Vietnamese to flee their homeland for resettlement abroad. In most cases a complex set of factors are involved—some on the "push" side and others on the "pull" side. Views differ on the relative weight that should be attached to these two sides of the refugee equation. The Songkhla analysis presented below gives greater weight to the "pull" side. Though some will disagree with this finding, the report represents an effort to analyze the present refugee flow based on interviews at the Songkhla camp.

In recounting the dreadful risks associated with the flight by boat, the report hints at the root cause of the problem – conditions and policies within Vietnam which produce sufficient unhappiness and desperation to lead large numbers of people to risk robbery, rape and death in a search for a new beginning. Also attached is a comment on the whole problem as the refugee section sees it over time. Whatever the various motivations of the boat refugees and our analysis of the composition of the flow, the central issue is that U.S. and third country resettlement programs remain the only way of preserving temporary asylum.

B. Text of Songkhla Message

1. Vietnamese refugee arrivals in southern Thailand over the past three months have been at approximately the same levels as a year ago with no indication of a slackening. Conversations with recently arrived refugees at the Songkhla camp confirm that many more Vietnamese are preparing to leave by boat for a new life in the West at their first opportunity. To make that journey, Vietnamese must undergo the hazardous boat crossing via the Gulf of Thailand to Songkhla or any other destination. Such a voyage means almost certain robbery, rape or worse at the hands of the hundreds of fishermen-pirates who prey upon Vietnamese refugees. Nature's own risks compound the danger, as many boats and lives are lost to the sea itself. Despite these known risks, the flow of refugees seems destined to continue at its current level. Indeed, those closely associated with the refugee problem have told me they anticipate the refugee flow continuing at high levels for several years into the future.

Given the importance of the Indochinese refugee program to U.S. foreign policy, it is essential to understand why this outpouring of Vietnamese boat refugees continues. To probe

refugee motivation, I have spoken extensively with Vietnamese boat refugees, American and foreign government officials
working with the refugees, members of private voluntary
agencies closely associated with refugee assistance and resettlement, and with representatives of international organ-
izations. The result of this examination is a snapshot view of
the current Vietnamese boat arrivals in southern Thailand. As
such it should not be used as a basis for extrapolation to other
groups and/or time periods.

2. The motivations of those leaving Vietnam and coming
to southern Thailand can be as varied and complex as the
individuals themselves, making categorizations difficult.
Perhaps this was not so in the immediate aftermath of the
Vietnam war, when fears of the new rulers of the south provided a clear impetus to the mass exodus of those associated
with the old regime or its American allies. While the chaos
in South Vietnam has not subsided entirely, it does seem to
have reached a level where we can now look somewhat more
discerningly at the question of motivation. In so doing, one
finds the spectrum of motivation ranges from those who are
truly fleeing from obvious and intense political persecution
at the hands of the new Vietnamese Government to those
who simply want to leave for what they perceive as a more
prosperous life in the United States. Between these two
extremes there remain many refugees whose motives are
mixed and less readily identifiable. With the above caveats
in mind, certain general conclusions can be drawn about
the relative strengths of specific considerations which lead
Vietnamese to become boat refugees.

3. At one end of the spectrum, there are what can only be
described as political refugees. Those among recent arrivals

affiliated with the former government's now discredited civil or military bureaucracy indeed have no future in their native country. They have been systematically deprived of their political, economic and social rights with little chance that these lost human rights can be recouped. Many of those in this category who reach Songkhla have only recently been released from "re-education camps" or escaped from "new economic zones". Others are family members of those who cannot leave such places or have died in them, and who have been so tarred by that family association that they have no future in their own homeland. For these people there is little alternative but to escape Vietnam and seek a new life. In years past, these people may well have represented a majority of those coming out. Today, however, they are a definite minority of those arriving in Songkhla camp—at most twenty percent.

4. At another end of the spectrum are those refugees who are most accurately described as economic emigrants, leaving Vietnam for the same reasons that have impelled immigrants towards America for generations. Economic conditions in Vietnam are, by all accounts from refugees, harsh and deteriorating rather than stabilizing. Under such circumstances it should not be surprising that at least one-half of all newly arrived refugees in Songkhla give as their primary motive for leaving Vietnam the desire to seek a better economic life for themselves and their children in the United States. When initially questioned, most of these refugees state that they left Vietnam because they hate "Communism" and want to live in "freedom".

Closer questioning, however, as to what anti-Communism and freedom mean for these refugees reveals that they are actually talking about economic betterment. They reveal no indication of having been singled out for discriminatory treatment in any manner. People in this category were invariably employed in Vietnam, usually as unskilled or semi-skilled labor, and were making a living with adequate food and consumer goods available. They complain, however, about high prices and the need to deal frequently on the black market where such goods are expensive. Their clear motivation is to reach the United States, have better jobs, make more money, buy more consumer goods, and live better than in Vietnam. Were these people less certain of resettlement in the U.S., or if their economic prospects in Vietnam were significantly better, they would have remained at home rather than risk the crossing to Songkhla.

5. For those remaining thirty percent or so refugees, motivations are somewhat more complex and difficult to sort out exactly. For example, ethnic background complicates the question. For the ethnic Chinese who make up about ten percent of current Songkhla arrivals, one might plausibly argue that they are victims of officially sanctioned economic discrimination, and that by expressing a desire for economic betterment they are in fact fleeing an associated political injustice. Tempering this view, however, is the fact that the Chinese themselves, invariably express their own motives in economic terms unless they were part of the very few Chinese associated with the old regime.

Another complicating factor in determining motivation is age. At least half of all draft age young men fleeing Vietnam appear to be doing so, at least in large part, to avoid military conscription and an unpopular war in Cambodia. Another motivation is certainly family reunification. Nearly all of the refugees claim to have relatives of varying degrees of closeness in the United States. In many cases fleeing Vietnam is a matter of spouses or children seeking to reunite with those who have gone before to the United States. Certainly, the family motivation is strong in such cases, tempering the underlying economic motivation which these refugees also express. Obviously, there are numerous other factors which dilute or modify what might otherwise be classified solely as economic motivation.

6. For those fleeing clear political persecution, that which they flee is in itself probably sufficient cause to take nearly any risk to escape. But what about the others? Can economic motivation in itself provide a strong enough impetus to risk apprehension by Vietnamese security forces, piracy, rape and drowning at sea to seek a better life in the West? Perhaps by itself, such an economic motivation does not. To the economic impetus, however, one must add certain factors and perceptions of the would-be refugees. The most important of these is the almost certain knowledge that they will be resettled in the United States. They know the size of our yearly refugee admissions quota as well as details of the category system to determine eligibility. Moreover, they know how to work the system to their best advantage. If by some stroke of bad fortune they are unable to get to the U.S., they know that some other Western country will take them instead.

Closely related to this first perception is confidence that they will make it safely to Thailand as their first stop. They recognize that they will probably be robbed or raped, but such misfortune is simply calculated—as is the boat passage fee—as part of the costs of getting to the United States. And, once in Thailand, their stay in Songkhla will be brief due to rapid and efficient processing by U.S. agencies. The normal stay in Songkhla camp is now approximately two months, a fact well-known to would-be refugees.

7. Nearly every refugee reaching Songkhla at this time has a relative already in the United States. Approximately half of those relatives are newly arrived refugees themselves, having arrived in the U.S. within the past three months to one year. Clearly what is happening is a phenomenon whereby one family member will escape from Vietnam and seek admission to the United States, not even asking for resettlement elsewhere for fear of being accepted. Once resettled in the U.S., the first member notifies his relatives still in Vietnam that they can then make their escape. Following family members can then leave confident that they will fall into a high enough category to be eligible for quick resettlement in the United States.

In short, when the potential refugee is contemplating leaving Vietnam, he knows that he will be pirated, that his women will be raped, and that there is some chance he will lose his life at sea. Yet balancing this knowledge is the belief that at the end of his voyage there is almost guaranteed resettlement in the United States. These perceptions provide a powerful impetus for any dissatisfied Vietnamese to leave their native country, whatever their other motives. The vortex effect is obvious. Family members leave Vietnam, reach the U.S., send money and good news, thereby encouraging more family members to leave. They, in turn, are related to still other potential immigrants, their numbers increasing geometrically much like recipients of a chain letter. Gibson.

C. Refugee Section Comment:
1. Boat refugees are leaving Vietnam for a variety of reasons. We continue to see a significant proportion of political refugees, some fresh out of prison or re-education. Others, including members of the middle-class, former civil and military personnel, students and the Chinese flee because they see an

utterly hopeless future. Such individuals constitute 3/4 of the U.S./boat refugee caseload in Thailand. Some might term such refugees "economic" but to the extent that they are from segments of society being systematically and intentionally defined out of the new Communist system, they are victims of the political policies of the SRV.

There is a smaller proportion of people of more ordinary background who may have had the opportunity for some marginal niche in the Communist economic system, and who may more closely fit the "economic" label, but even these people are desperate enough to risk the boat trip.

2. Enough is generally known about the extraordinary dangers and terrors of being a boat refugee so that we will not dwell on it. The prospect of rape for women refugees is omnipresent and the sailing conditions of some boats are simply incredible.

3. The statistics cited in AmConsul Songkhla message apparently relate to observations about the overall boat refugee population. More precise statistics are available for that portion of refugees accepted by the U.S. program and shed a bit more light on the flow which is not predominantly lower class, and includes a large percentage who do not have U.S. relatives:

- Former professionals, middle class, students and government officials – 75 percent (about a third of whom are Chinese)
- Those with close relatives in U.S. (through siblings) – about 20 percent
- Those with distant relatives in U.S. – about 40 percent
- Former farmers, fishermen, laborers – about 20 percent.

4. Without doubt the U.S. and third country resettlement programs do have a magnetic effect. Yet dissatisfaction and hopelessness are so pervasive in Vietnam that many refugees would continue to flee even if it meant an indefinite stay in refugee camps. This would not be a totally unacceptable outcome, but the problem is that without resettlement offtake the temporary asylum countries would soon close their doors.

Our belief (shared by most of those who screen and interview the refugees) that many refugees would opt to leave Vietnam even for an indefinite stay in the refugee camps, sharply distinguishes the boat refugee flow from a migrant stream. In other words, even in the absence of "pull factors," "push factors" would continue to drive many Vietnamese on to refugee boats.

Appendix 3

Extract from the UNHCR report State of the World's Refugees 2000 – https://www.unhcr.org/3ebf9bad0.html

Piracy in the South China Sea.

Piracy in Southeast Asia is as old as seafaring itself. For the Vietnamese 'boat people' it posed an unexpected terror and for those seeking to protect them it was a vexing problem. In 1981 alone, when 452 boats arrived in Thailand carrying 15,479 refugees, UNHCR's statistics were a study in horror: 349 boats had been attacked an average of three times each; 578 women had been raped; 228 women had been abducted; and 881 people were dead or missing.

The anti-piracy programme

Responding to mounting international outrage and a demand for action, UNHCR launched a fund-raising appeal at the end of 1981. By June 1982, an anti-piracy programme was officially begun with US$3.6 million in funding from 12 countries. In Thailand, anti-piracy efforts initially focused on sea and air patrols, which produced a gradual decline in the number of attacks.

However, as High Commissioner Poul Hartling noted at the time: 'Even if the quantity has gone down, the quality of the attacks, if you can say that, is going up ... What we hear is even more horrifying than in the past.' The reports 'tell of cruelty, brutality and inhumanity that go beyond my imagination. The refugees are attacked with knives and clubs. There is murder, robbery and rape, everything in this world.'

From 1984, the UNHCR anti-piracy programme shifted increasingly toward land-based operations. Thai police units and harbour officials registered fishing boats, photographed crews, and conducted public awareness campaigns on the penalties for piracy. UNHCR helped to link piracy victims with police and prosecutors, monitored court trials, arranged witness transfers from abroad, and provided interpretation services for investigations, arrests and trials. By 1987, only eight per cent of all boats arriving in Thailand were attacked. There were abductions and rape but no reported deaths due to piracy.

In 1988, however, the violence of the attacks began to rise alarmingly again, with more than 500 people reported dead or missing. In 1989, this number exceeded 750. Rapes and abductions spiralled upward.

In August 1989, one UNHCR official who debriefed the survivors of one attack, described how the pirates brought up men singly from the hold, clubbed them and then killed them with axes. Vietnamese in the water were then rammed, sunk and killed, leaving 71 people dead, including 15 women and 11 children. The rise in violence at sea, anti-piracy experts suggested, was due in part to the success of the land-based efforts. More sophisticated investigations were leading to higher rates of arrest and conviction. This was scaring off the occasional opportunists but leaving behind a hard core of professional criminals who, in turn, wished to leave behind no witnesses.

Eventually, it seems that even they tired of the chase.

After mid-1990, there were no more reports of pirate attacks on Vietnamese boats, and in December 1991 the UNHCR anti-piracy programme was discontinued. 'The war on the pirates is not over', said the final assessment report, 'but it has reached the stage where it can be effectively managed' by local agencies.

Rescue at sea

From 1975 to late 1978, 110,000 Vietnamese boat people arrived in first-asylum countries. At first, ship captains seemed eager to aid boats in distress and during these three years ships from 31 different countries rescued refugees from a total of 186 boats.

In August 1979, UNHCR convened a meeting in Geneva on the subject of rescue at sea. Out of these discussions came a programme known as DISERO (Disembarkation Resettlement Offers). Under this programme, eight Western states including the United States jointly agreed to guarantee resettlement for any Vietnamese refugee rescued at sea by merchant ships flying the flags of states that did not resettle refugees.

The new commitments appeared to have an almost immediate effect. In the last five months of 1979, 81 boats carrying 4,031 people were rescued at sea. In May 1980, UNHCR donated an unarmed speedboat to the Thai government in a token effort to bolster sea patrolling. Meanwhile, some of the private international mercy ships, including most prominently the Kap Anamur and the Ile de Lumière, shifted their operations from resupply of island camps to boat rescue.

Altogether, 67,000 Vietnamese were rescued at sea between 1975 and 1990. The problem with this programme was that the guarantee that any Vietnamese rescued at sea would be resettled within 90 days did not square with the

1989 Comprehensive Plan of Action guidelines, which required that all new arrivals undergo screening to determine their status.

Eventually, both DISERO and a later companion programme known as RASRO (Rescue at Sea Resettlement Offers) were terminated as countries in the region proved unwilling to disembark rescued boat people."